POP

Word 6.0

for Windows

PRISMA Computer Courses are structured, practical guides to mastering the most popular computer programs.
PRISMA books are course books, giving step-by-step instructions, which take the user through basic skills to advanced functions in easy to follow, manageable stages.

Now available:

dBase IV
Excel 4.0 for Windows
Lotus 1-2-3
Lotus 1-2-3 for Windows
MS-DOS
Novell Netware
UNIX
Windows
WordPerfect
WordPerfect for Windows
Visual Basic for Windows

Joachim Röhl, Johannes Verhuven

Word 6.0 for Windows

PRISMA COMPUTER COURSE

Prisma Computer Courses first published in Great Britain 1992 by

Het Spectrum
PO Box 2996
London N5 2TA

Translation: George Hall
Production: LINE UP text productions

© 1994 Rowohlt Taschenbuch Verlag GmbH, Reinbek bei Hamburg

For the English translation
© 1994 Uitgeverij Het Spectrum BV, Utrecht

ISBN 1 85365 395 0

British Library Cataloguing-in-Publication Data.
A catalogue record for this book is available from the British Library.

Contents

Foreword

The Word for Windows word processor is one of the best-selling Windows applications. The package provides many facilities for use in both professional and private areas. For instance, the package can be used to:

- create text and give it an attractive layout
- create a standard design for correspondence
- place headers and footers in your texts
- automatically place and edit footnotes in your texts
- draw up invoices
- create and print form letters
- create and apply special layout styles

These are only a few of the many facilities dealt with in this book. All example texts shown have been made using Word for Windows version 6.0. Among the many advantages provided by this program are:

- ease of operation
- simple data exchange with other Windows applications
- extensive possibilities
- favourable price/quality relationship.

Because all Windows applications are operated in more or less the same manner, the investment of time and energy in learning one application (such as Word) repays itself many times over when you come to deal with other Windows applications. You can then make optimum use of the Windows environment.

This book has been compiled as follows:

- Chapter 1 gives a brief outline of the benefits provided by Word for Windows, and states the system requirements.
- Chapter 2 describes the Word for Windows screen display in detail.
- Chapter 3 discusses how to make use of the Word

for Windows help function.

- Chapter 4 deals with the standard settings for the screen layout which you use in subsequent examples.
- Chapter 5 discusses the basic skills for creating and editing text.
- Chapter 6 deals with formatting (giving specific features to) separate characters, paragraphs and documents. Attention is given to direct formatting, formatting using the *Format* menu, the Ruler, the Formatting toolbar and the Standard toolbar. Text is divided into columns and the page is assigned a particular layout corresponding to the settings of the connected printer.
- Chapter 7 deals with the standard layout for correspondence.
- Chapter 8 goes further into text layout features.
- Chapter 9 deals with utilities for compiling texts, including the AutoCorrect feature which can automatically rectify mistakes made when typing text.
- Chapter 10 discusses headers and footers for above and below your texts; the footnote function is indispensible if you are working with scientific articles or articles which require acknowledgements and references.
- Chapter 11 deals with self-defined tab stops.
- Chapters 12 and 13 discuss using sections of text and form letters; once you master the functions dealt with here, your speed and efficiency will increase dramatically.
- Chapter 14 deals with creating and using specified layout styles.

In line with the other books in the *Compact Computer Course* series, we shall adhere to the following principles:

- The subject matter is presented in a way which is clear and easy to understand, even for a novice.
- We always begin with a clearly specified task.
- All examples can be directly worked out on the computer.
- The subject matter is relevant to daily usage.

1   Basic skills

1.1   The advantages of Word for Windows

Word is a word processor which has been developed specially for use under Windows. The program operation conforms to the standard Windows method of operation. This standard method means that all Windows applications have a similar menu structure, which ensures that you can also learn other Windows programs quickly and easily, such as Excel or Works, once you have learned how to work with Word.

Word for Windows is a graphic-oriented program. Text appears on the screen in the same way as it comes out of the printer. This type of display is referred to as WYSIWYG: What You See Is What You Get. This is further supported by a great number of so-called *True-Type fonts*, which are also identical on screen and paper. The package contains a large number of these fonts.

1.2   System requirements

In order to be able to work with the Word for Windows program, you need a personal computer with the MS-DOS operating system, on which Windows version 3.1 or higher has been installed. Powerful programs such as Word for Windows make severe demands on the processor. To work with Word for Windows you require at least an 80286 processor (but higher is better).

Working memory must have a capacity of at least 4 Mb, but to get the best out of the program 8 Mb is preferable. The disk capacity required depends on the type of installation you perform. You will need at least 3 Mb, but if you install all the Word for Windows components, approximately 25 Mb will be occupied.

The processing speed depends on the harddisk access time with some functions. A harddisk with an access time of 20 ms or less will reduce waiting time.

To install programs, a floppy diskdrive is necessary. Nowadays, most computers are equipped with a 3.5 inch diskdrive. A 5.25 inch diskdrive is also very useful to provide full compatibility when exchanging diskettes.

A keyboard (AT compatible) and a mouse (preferably Microsoft compatible) are required for text input and operation of the program. Windows and therefore Word for Windows work on all common display cards, such as VGA for instance. A colour monitor makes working with the computer a great deal more pleasant.

The so-called *printer drivers* are provided along with Windows. These are the operating programs required to run almost all printers which are currently on the market. In order to be able to use all the facilities provided by Word for Windows, you will need at least a 24-pin matrix printer; an inkjet or laser printer provides far better quality.

1.3   Installation

Word for Windows must be installed using the Setup program which is supplied along with Windows. This installation is implemented using menus. In addition to the program files, you can also copy the following files to the harddisk:

- spelling check
- thesaurus
- demonstrations of the new facilities in Word
- example files for texts, macros and templates
- filters for importing documents and objects from other applications
- utility programs such as the Comparison Editor.

When the Setup program has been concluded, the

Word for Windows program is stored on the harddisk in the directory you specified during installation. The system configuration takes place in Windows. If, for example, you connect another printer, specify the required settings via Windows. These will then automatically apply to all your Windows programs.

1.4   Starting Word under Windows

When Word has been installed, the program will be shown in the Microsoft Office or Microsoft Word 6.0 group window of the Program Manager. The programs in this program group are displayed along with their icons. You can start up Word by placing the mouse pointer on the Microsoft Word icon and double clicking (pressing twice in rapid succession) the left mouse button.

It is also possible to start up Word for Windows directly from DOS. In that case, type the following behind the DOS prompt:

```
win winword
```

Confirm this command by pressing Enter. The command 'win' starts up the Windows program and 'winword' activates the Word for Windows program. You will arrive directly in Word for Windows without an interim stop at the Program Manager.

If you start up the program in this way, it is also possible to load text files by specifying parameters behind the commands.

When loading a particular text, the following syntax applies:

```
win winword diskdrive:\directory\filename
```

For example:
When Word has been started up, the LETTER1.DOC text file in the C:\PRIVATE directory is to be loaded. To do this in one go, give the following command:

```
win winword c:\private\letter1.doc
```

You do not need to specify the drive and directory if the file is located on the currently active drive and in the currently active directory.

Exercise 1

1   Which advantages does Word for Windows provide for the user?

_____

_____

_____

_____

_____

2   Enter the missing text:

Word is a _____ program. A text is shown on the screen just as it will come out of _____. This type of display is known as _____.

3   What are the system requirements of Word?

Processor: _____

Working memory capacity: _____

Harddisk capacity: _____

4   Do you have to specify the graphic card, the
    mouse, keyboard and printer during the Word in-
    stallation?

    _____

    _____

5   Imagine that you want to start up Word directly
    from DOS and want to load the PRACTICE docu-
    ment straightaway. Write down the commands you
    should type.

    _____

    _____

    _____

Answers 1

1   Which advantages does Word for Windows pro-
    vide for the user?

    *Word is a word processing program which has
    been specially developed for use under Windows.
    It is operated in the standard Windows way. Since
    all other Windows programs are also operated in
    this manner, the operation method is quickly
    learned.*

2   Enter the missing text:

    Word is a *graphic-oriented* program. A text is
    shown on the screen just as it will come out of *the
    printer.* This type of display is known as
    WYSIWYG (What You See Is What You Get).

3   What are the system requirements of Word?

    Processor: *at least 80286, preferably 80386 or
    80486*
    Working memory capacity: *at least 4 Mb, prefer-
    ably 8 Mb*
    Harddisk capacity: *approximately 26 Mb for a com-
    plete installation.*

4   Do you have to specify the graphic card, the
    mouse, keyboard and printer during the Word in-
    stallation?

    *No, that occurs during the installation of Windows
    itself.*

5   Imagine that you want to start up Word directly
    from DOS and want to load the PRACTICE docu-
    ment straightaway. Write down the commands you
    should type.

    win winword practice

2 The opening screen

At the start of Word, the following screen appears:

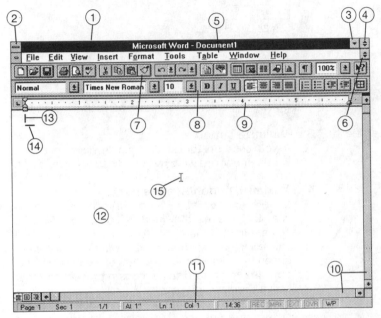

The screen contains the following elements:

1   Title bar
This contains the name of the Windows program, in this case 'Microsoft Word' and the name of the text. If no existing document has yet been opened, Word automatically assigns the temporary name 'Document1'.

2   The Control menu
A menu is concealed behind this symbol. You can open it by clicking on it using the mouse or by pressing the key combination Alt-Spacebar.

You can activate Windows functions by means of this menu. For example, it is possible to alter the size of the window, to end the Word session and to switch to a different Windows program.

3   Minimize button
If you click on the small triangle pointing downwards, the Word window is reduced to an icon.

4   Maximize button/Restore button
If there are two triangles at the right button position, this means the window completely fills the screen. In that case, the Restore button is active. If you click on this button, the window will be reduced to roughly three quarters of the screen. This provides room to display icons representing other active Windows programs.
If there is only one triangle pointing upwards at the right button position (Maximize button), a click on this button will enlarge the window to fill the screen.

5   Menu bar
The Control menu button for the *document window* is located at the left-hand side of the menu bar. You can open the menu by clicking on the button or by pressing the key combination Alt-Hyphen. The menus on the menu bar can also be opened using the mouse or by pressing a key combination consisting of the Alt key together with the underlined letter of the required option. For instance, the File menu is opened by pressing Alt-F. This menu contains various commands. When you open a menu, a list of options opens up. You use these

options to start functions or specify settings. The Help menu is situated at the extreme right of the menu bar. This opens the integrated Help function.

6   Restore button/Maximize button for the document window
The Restore button/Maximize button for the document window is located at the right of the menu bar. This enables you to display the document in a separate window.

7   Standard toolbar
The standard toolbar has been specially developed for the mouse. The most important functions, such as opening documents, copying, cutting, pasting and printing, can be executed by means of these icons.

When you place the mouse pointer on a button without clicking, the name of the button appears in a small frame. The status bar will then provide a brief description of the button function. The following buttons are shown on the standard toolbar, from left to right:

☐	New	Open a new document
☞	Open	Open an existing document
💾	Save	Save a document
🖨	Print	Print a text
🔍	Print Preview	Switch to the Print Preview window

	Spelling	Activate the spelling check
	Cut	Cut out a section of text and copy it to the Clipboard
	Copy	Copy a section of text to the Clipboard
	Paste	Insert a section of text from the Clipboard
	Format Painter	Copy and Paste a certain format
	Undo	Undo the previous action(s); not all actions can be undone
	Redo	Restore the actions just undone
	AutoFormat	Apply automatic formatting
	Insert AutoText	Insert text in the document
	Insert Table	Insert a table in the text
	Insert Microsoft Excel worksheet	Insert a Microsoft Excel worksheet in the document
	Columns	Divide the text into columns
	Drawing	Activate the Drawing Toolbar

	Insert Chart	Insert a chart into the text (Microsoft Graph utility program)
	Show/Hide ¶	Display non-printable characters in the document on the screen.
100%	Zoom Control	Alter the size of the document on the screen
	Help	Activate the context-oriented Help function

8 Formatting toolbar

Using the Formatting toolbar you can specify settings for the layout, the fonts, the font size and the common character and paragraph layout features.

If you place the mouse pointer on a button without clicking, the name of the button appears in a small frame. The following buttons appear on the Formatting toolbar, from left to right:

	Style	Options list of all styles defined for the document
	Font	Options list of all available fonts
	Font Size	Options list of all available font sizes
B	Bold	Place text in boldface
I	Italic	Place text in italics

U	Underline	Have text underlined
	Align Left	Left-align text
	Center	Centre a paragraph
	Align Right	Right-align text
	Justify	Align text both left and right
	Numbering	Compile numbered lists
	Bullets	Summary characters
	Decrease Indent	Reduce line indentation by one tabstop
	Increase Indent	Increase line indentation by one tabstop
	Borders	Activate the Borders toolbar

9   Ruler
The Ruler enables you to specify settings for formatting paragraphs and page margins. Tabstops can be set using the mouse. The individual possibilities for text layout will be dealt with in the relevant sections.

10   Scroll bars
Normally the display of both scroll bars is activated. The vertical scroll bar enables you to browse through a text. The horizontal scroll bar enables you to examine sections of text which are too wide to fit onto the screen. Where applicable we shall indicate the various facilities for shifting text on the screen.
The following buttons are situated on the horizontal scroll bar:

These buttons have the following functions, from left to right:

	Normal View	Show the document on screen in normal display
	Page Layout View	Show the document as pages in real size on the screen
	Outline View	Show the document in outline view on the screen

11 Status bar
The following information is given on the status bar:

The current insertion point:

Page 1	Page 1
Sec 1	Section 1
1/1	First page of a total of one page(s)
At 1"	Current distance from the top edge of the paper
Ln 1	Current line position
Col 1	Current column position
11:44	Current system time

Additional information:

REC	The Macro recorder is running
MRK	Revision marking is active
EXT	Extend mode is active (F8)
OVR	The Typeover mode is active
WP	Help information for WordPerfect users is active

If the computer reacts unexpectedly, check if certain modes have been activated. When you open a menu, a short description of the facilities provided by the menu is given on the status bar. You can read these by moving to each option using the cursor keys (clicking will activate the option immediately).

12 Document window
This is where you type and edit the text.

13 Insertion point
This is a blinking vertical stripe at the position where text can be entered.

14 End mark
The end of a text is marked by a horizontal stripe.

15 Mouse pointer
The shape of the mouse pointer indicates which actions can be carried out using the mouse. If the mouse is in the document window, it is shown as a vertical stripe with two short horizontal bars (the *I beam*). In that case, you can determine the insertion position using the mouse. On the menu bar, the toolbars and the Ruler, the mouse pointer has the form of an arrow pointing diagonally left. In the text boxes on the toolbars, the mouse pointer has the same shape as the insertion point in the text window. In the selection area at the left-hand side of the screen, the mouse pointer assumes the form of an arrow pointing to the right. In this case, you can easily select (mark) lines or paragraphs, for instance.

Exercise 2

1   Place a cross next to the correct statements:

■   The title bar shows the name of the Windows program and the name of the current document.   ☐

- The Control menu can only be opened using the mouse. ☐
- The Control menu contains Windows functions. ☐
- If you click on the Minimize button, the Word window will be reduced to an icon; the Program Manager will then become active. ☐
- You always make the Word window screen-filling by means of the Restore/Maximize button. ☐
- The menu bar displays only the names of the menus which you can open using the mouse or by pressing Alt along with the underlined letter. ☐
- You can only format characters using the Formatting toolbar. ☐
- Among other things, the Ruler is used for formatting paragraphs. ☐
- Information about the insertion point, the display mode, the activation of special keys and menu options is given on the status bar. ☐

2   The shape of the mouse pointer provides information about its function. Which function does the mouse pointer have when it looks like this?:

I

_____
_____
_____

R

_____
_____
_____

Answers 2

1   Place a cross next to the correct statements:

■ The title bar shows the name of the Windows program and the name of the current document.   ☒

■ The Control menu can only be opened using the mouse.   ☐

■ The Control menu contains Windows functions.   ☒

■ If you click on the Minimize button, the Word window will be reduced to an icon; the Program Manager will then become active.   ☒

■ You always make the Word window screen-filling by means of the Restore/Maximize button.   ☐

■ The menu bar displays only the names of the menus which you can open using the mouse or by pressing Alt along with the underlined letter.   ☐

■ You can on;y format characters using the Formatting toolbar.   ☐

■ Among other things, the Ruler is used for formatting paragraphs.   ☒

■ Information about the insert position, the display mode, the activation of special keys and menu options is given on the status bar.   ☐

2   The shape of the mouse pointer provides information about its function. Which function does it have when it looks like this:

Ⅰ

The mouse pointer is in the document window; the insertion point can be moved by clicking on the left mouse button.

On the menu bar, the toolbars and the Ruler, the mouse pointer assumes the shape of an arrow pointing leftwards; you can use it to select options from these components.

3 Quick information about commands

3.1 The Help menu

Not only beginners but also advanced users have difficulty finding the appropriate function now and again. Word Provides help by means of the Help menu.

You can activate this help in various ways. If you are using the keyboard, press the Alt key, hold it down and press the (underlined) H from the Help menu. If you are working with the mouse, move the mouse pointer to the Help menu on the menu bar and click once on the left button.

The *Help* menu provides the following functions:

Contents
Gives an overview of the Help function.

Search for Help on...
Type a search word in the text box. The topics related to this search word will appear in the Search dialog window. You can quickly switch to the required topic.

Index
The key words of the available topics are shown in the Index.

Quick Preview
This option provides demonstrations of new Word facilities.

Examples and Demos
As the name indicates, this option provides help about a chosen topic in the form of graphically illustrated examples.

Tip of the Day
Displays a new tip each Day, which you will see when Word is started up; it is possible to browse through available tips.

WordPerfect Help
Provides a list of WordPerfect features and their equivalents in Word.

Technical support
Provides a summary of technical help in the form of information and addresses you can consult if you encounter problems.

About Microsoft Word
Provides information about the license, copyright and version and also gives access to detailed system information.

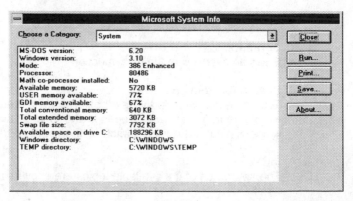

If you want to learn how to work with the Help function, select *Search for Help on....* from the Help menu. You can activate this option by moving the cursor bar to it and pressing Enter, by pressing the underlined letter (S) or by clicking on it using the mouse.

Example
Select Search for Help on... from the Help menu.

The Word Help window appears. This window has a title and a menu bar. You can specify a search word in the text box in the dialog window. You can also select the required key word from the options list. Pressing Tab switches to the options list where you can select a key word using the cursor keys. You can also browse through the various key words using the mouse and the scroll bar.

Example
Select the key word 'Help'.

Click on the *Show Topics* button to display the related topics in the section in the lower part of the window. Activating the *Go To* button will produce information about one of the topics shown.

Example
We shall select the topic 'fonts, changing' because we wish to know more about which types of letters we can use for our documents.

- Select *Search for Help on* from the *Help* menu.
- Go to the options list by pressing Tab or by clicking on the scrollbar.
- Highlight 'fonts, changing' and click on the Show Topics button.
- Click on 'Changing the default character formatting' option in the lower section of the window.
- Click on the Go To button.

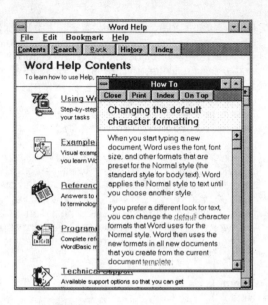

The help window displays information about the character formatting.

It is also possible to print this information so that it is readily available when you are working. Click on the Print button in the How To window. If your printer is properly connected, the appropriate text should appear.

It is also possible to print text from the Word Help window itself. Open the *File* menu in this window and select *Print Topic*.

In the Word Help window there are three buttons under the menu bar. These have the following significance:

Contents   This button switches you to the Word Help: Contents window. This is the window which appears when you select the *Contents* option from the *Help* menu.

Search	This button enables you to search for certain terms or problems.
Back	This button activates the previous help screen.
History	The History window shows the help topics which have been previously activated.
Index	Provides an overview of the key words for various help topics.

In the case of large help texts which occupy more than one page, a vertical scroll bar appears automatically so that you can browse through the text.
In the help text there are terms which are underlined with a dotted line. All defined terms in Word are underlined with a dotted line. If you click on one of these terms, a small window with an explanation of that term will appear within the current window. This small window is closed again by clicking anywhere outside It.

At the bottom of the Help window, you may see underlined references under **See Also** to topics related to the topic in the currently active help window. By clicking on one of these, you can switch to the corresponding topic.

Example
We shall switch to the Using Word window.

This is done by clicking on the underlined line 'Using Word' in the Word Help window. Using the mouse and the scroll bar, you can browse through the various topics in the Using Word window. If you click on a scroll arrow, the window is shifted up or down one line. If you click on the scroll bar itself, the text is moved one screen page. The small block in the scroll bar indicates how far the text has moved in relation to the total size of the text. You can also use this block to browse through the text. Place the mouse pointer on the scroll

block and drag the block a certain distance by holding
down the left mouse button. Release the mouse button
when you see the required text on the screen.

Close the Help function by selecting *Exit* from the *File*
menu.

3.2   The context-oriented Help function

You will probably need a little help now and again. To
get help on a specific topic, select the required option
using the cursor keys (not the mouse!) and press F1.
This is the way to activate the context-oriented Help
function. If you press F1 again, the 'Contents for How
to Use Help' window is opened.

Example
Highlight the *Options* option in the *Tools* menu. Press
F1 to activate the corresponding help window.

You can also press Shift-F1 to activate the Help function. A question mark is now attached to the mouse
pointer.

Note: If during the installation you have opted for an active 'Help for WordPerfect Users' function, information
about WordPerfect will appear on the screen when you
press the Shift-F1 key combination. You can activate
and deactivate this option by opening the *Tools* menu,
selecting *Options*, clicking on the General tab sheet to
activate it. Clicking on the Help for WordPerfect Users
check box will activate (cross) and deactivate (no
cross) this option.

We shall presume that the Help for WordPerfect Users
option has been deactivated. If you now want to know
more about an element on the screen, press Shift-F1,
move the mouse pointer to the element in question and
press the left mouse button. For instance, if you click
on the Formatting toolbar, the toolbar help window will

be opened. In this way, you can also gain information about key combinations. Imagine you want to know more about the key combination Alt-F4 (closing Word). Proceed as follows:

■ Press Shift-F1: the question mark appears alongside the mouse pointer.
■ Press Alt-F4: the 'Exit command' help window appears (this is a command in the *File* menu).

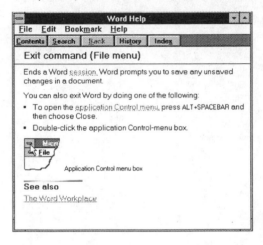

Exercise 3

1 While working with Word, you want to gain information about the various components of the status bar. How do you do this?

_____
_____
_____

2 You want to read the available texts concerning the topic 'changing window sizes'. How do you display the available topics on the screen?

_____
_____
_____
_____
_____

3   You want to gain information about the third icon
    on the Standard toolbar. How do you display the
    relevant information?

_____
_____

Answers 3

1   While working with Word, you want to gain infor-
    mation about the various components of the status
    bar. How do you do this?

    *Press Shift-F1 or click with the mouse on the
    question mark icon on the Standard toolbar. Then
    move the mouse pointer to the status bar and
    press the left mouse button.*

2   You want to read the available texts concerning
    the topic 'changing window sizes'. How do you dis-
    play the available topics on the screen?

    *Select the Search For Help On command from the
    Help menu. Type 'window' in the text box of the
    Search dialog window. Display the available topics
    by means of the Show Topics button and select
    the 'Sizing a window' option from the appropriate
    box.*

3   You want to gain information about the third icon
    on the Standard toolbar. How do you display the
    relevant information?

    *Press Shift-F1 or click on the question mark icon
    on the Standard toolbar. Move the mouse pointer
    to the third icon (showing the diskette) of the Stan-
    dard toolbar and click on the left mouse button.*

4 Changing the default settings

4.1 Mouse or keyboard

When describing the help windows in the previous chapter, we have indicated that you can use the mouse, the keyboard or key combinations (shortcut keys) to implement commands. The help windows are ideal for experimenting with these three methods since you cannot cause irreversible damage to the text. In fact, Word provides many ways of executing commands. Even the most fanatic mouse users make use of the keyboard to execute certain commands because this method is sometimes quicker or easier.

For this reason we shall describe how to use the keyboard to give instructions in the coming chapters. You can make up your own mind whether you want to use the keyboard or the mouse.

4.2 Changing the Word screen

When you start up Word for the first time, all components of the screen are actually shown: the title bar, menu bar, Standard toolbar, Formatting toolbar, Ruler, status bar and scroll bars. The toolbars and Ruler are convenient for text layout. However, you do need the Ruler when initially entering and editing text. You can temporarily remove it from the screen as follows:

- Open the *View* menu.
- Select *Ruler*.

The *Ruler* option has a tick in front of it in the menu. As soon as you choose this option, the tick is removed (although you can't see this because the menu is immediately closed). If you want to display the Ruler on the screen again, choose the *Ruler* option once more.

The *Options* option from the *Tools* menu opens a dialog window in which you can specify, via the View tab
sheet, settings which influence the screen display. You
can use the mouse or the cursor keys to activate any of
the tab sheets shown here. When a tab sheet has been
chosen, you can use the Tab key or the Alt key in combination with the underlined letter to open the required
section. An option is then activated or deactivated by
pressing the spacebar. Clicking with the mouse has the
same effect.

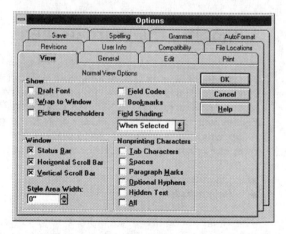

The options presented in the View, General, Edit and
Save tab sheets enable you to adjust the Word settings
to your own requirements.

The View tab sheet

The Show section of the View tab sheet enables you to determine whether or not the text is to be shown on the screen in the Draft Font. In addition, you can also limit the boundary of the text wrap to the width of the window. And if you include figures in your text, the Picture Placeholders option determines if the figure is to be shown completely or only with an indication of its position. By activating the options mentioned here, Word will work more quickly. However, the screen display does not entirely correspond to the result on paper.

You can also activate the Field Codes and the Bookmarks in this section. Fields can also be given extra emphasis by means of shading. Activate only the Field Codes option in this section for the moment.

The options in the Window section have the following functions:

Status Bar
Shows the status bar on screen. This is advisable because it provides information about your current working position in the text, about the control keys which are active or about the actions which are possible at any given moment etc.

Horizontal Scroll Bar
It is useful to have a horizontal scroll bar if the text is wider than the working area on the screen. This is the case, for example, when you are typing a text which has to be printed in Landscape Orientation (lengthwise).

Vertical Scroll Bar
This option activates a vertical scroll bar which is handy for lengthy texts.

Style Area Width
This option defines the width of a column at the left-hand side of the screen. It is not possible to type run-

ning text in this column. Once you are familiar with
Word, you can use this column to control text layout.
Specify the width of the layout area by typing a value in
the text box for this option or select the value by means
of the arrows.

We advise you to accept the default settings in this
Window section (see the figure).

The Nonprinting Characters section contains the following options:

Tab Characters
Tabs are not normally shown on screen. If you choose
this option, the tabs will be shown as arrowheads pointing right.

Spaces
If you want to see at a glance the amount of spaces between words, activate this option. The spaces are then
shown as dots.

Paragraph Marks
Paragraph marks are shown by means of the ¶ symbol
in the text. If you create a new line by pressing Shift-
Enter, this is represented by the ∏ character.

Optional Hyphens
In Word you can choose from a number of different
kinds of hyphens (for instance to prevent parts of a
whole being placed on different lines). If you activate
this option, the various hyphens are shown on the
screen using different symbols.

Hidden Text
If you have created some hidden text, you can show it
on the screen by means of this option.

All
This option displays *all* nonprinting characters on the
screen.

We advise you to activate the Tab Characters, Paragraph Marks, Optional Hyphens and Hidden Text options from this section.

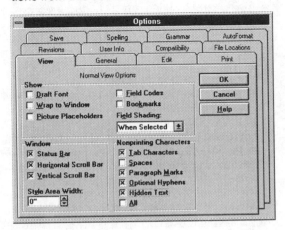

The General tab sheet

The General tab sheet options enable you to specify the general settings for the word processor and the units of measure.

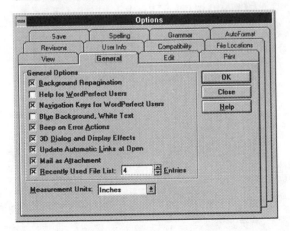

The various options have the following functions:

Background Repagination
If you are working on a text consisting of several pages, Word will automatically adjust the page breaks when you add or remove sections of text, unless you deactivate this option.

Help for WordPerfect Users
If you are accustomed to working with WordPerfect, you can activate this option to help facilitate the switch to Word. You can use the function keys as you are accustomed to in WordPerfect. Depending on the settings in the WordPerfect Help dialog window, either a demonstration of the function in Word will be displayed or a step-by-step description will be given.

Navigation Keys for WordPerfect Users
If this option is activated, the PgUp, PgDn, Home, End and Esc keys are allocated the functions they have in WordPerfect.

Blue Background, White Text
If you activate this option, the text is shown in white on a blue background.

Beep on Error Actions
If you press non-defined key combinations, Word will produce an acoustic signal.

3D Dialog and Display Effects
Tab sheets, dialog windows and buttons are shown with 3D effects.

Update Automatic Links at Open
If you import objects from other applications into a Word document (such as an Excel worksheet for example), the original document is compared to the contents of the Word document. If changes have been made to the original, the Word document is also updated. This occurs when the Word document is opened.

Mail as Attachment
This option is interesting when computers are working
together in a network and exchange documents.

Recently Used File List
If this option is activated, the files which were last used
are shown in the *File* menu. Accordingly, you can activate these files more quickly. A maximum of nine files
can be adopted into the *File* menu.

We advise you to activate the options Background Repagination, Beep on Error Actions and 3D Dialog and
Display Effects. Keep the Recently Used File List at the
default setting, 4.

Measurement Units
Normally Word works with inches in the English version. You can also work with centimetres, points or picas if you prefer.

The Edit tab sheet

Typing Replaces Selection
If you activate this option, you can select a passage of
text and type a new text which is then typed directly
over the selected text. This option can be very useful
when you have to make large-scale alterations to a document.

Drag-and-Drop Text Editing
When working with the mouse, this is a convenient option for moving a particular section of text. You select
the required passage and drag it wholly to the new position without having to make use of the Clipboard.

Automatic Word Selection
This options enables you to select entire words in one
go.

Use the INS Key for Paste
This option enables you to use the Ins key to insert the

contents of the Clipboard at the appropriate position. If this option is activated, it is not possible to use the Ins key to switch back and forwards between the insert and overtype modes.

Overtype mode
Also known as Typeover. If you activate this option, the text you type at the insertion point is typed over the existing text. Normally existing text shifts to the right when you type. The Ins key has the same function. If you have activated the Use the INS key for Paste option, you can use this option to switch back and forward between the insert and the overtype modes.

Use Smart Cut and Paste
When cutting out texts in Word, an automatic check is performed as to whether there are too many or too few spaces. When pasting a section of text, spaces are added to the beginning and end of the section if required.

Allow Accented Uppercase
If you activate this option, the program will ask whether or not capitals are to be given accents when you convert small letters to capitals, for instance when you are working in French (for example é becomes É).

We advise you to activate the options Typing Replaces Selection, Drag-and-Drop Text Editing and Use Smart Cut and Paste.

Picture Editor
This normally starts the Microsoft Word Picture Editor for working with closed figures. If other graphic programs are installed under Windows, you can select them instead.

The Save tab sheet

This tab sheet provides a large number of special options. Here is a summary of the options required for saving files:

Always Create Backup Copy
When you save a new version of a file, a backup of the
old version is made with the extension .BAK. If you
make a mess of the new version, you always have the
old one to fall back on.

Allow Fast Saves
This option is only important if the texts you are working on are rather lengthy. Word speeds up the saving
process by only writing to disk any alterations.

These two options cannot be active simultaneously.
We advise you to activate the Always Create Backup
Copy option.

Save Every *xx* minutes
Type the required number of minutes here. After the
specified time interval, Word makes an automatic
backup copy of your document. If a breakdown or dis-
turbance should occur, the loss of information will be
restricted.

We advise you to specify an interval of 5 or 10 minutes
here, depending on the rate of change.

Exercise 4

1   Which commands display and remove the Ruler?

   _____

   _____

2   When working with Word, you want to know which
    control keys are currently activated and also the
    exact position of the insertion point. Which option
    in the Options dialog window must be activated?

    Tab sheet: _____
    Section: _____
    Option: _____

3   Which options in the Nonprinting Characters sec-
    tion in the View tab sheet in the Options dialog
    window are advisable for normal word processing?
    Place a cross next to the appropriate options:

    ☐   Tab Characters
    ☐   Spaces
    ☐   Paragraph Marks
    ☐   Optional Hyphens
    ☐   Hidden Text
    ☐   All

4   Which options should be active in order to safe-
    guard the documents as much as possible?

    Menu: _____
    Command: _____
    Tab sheet: _____
    Option: _____
    Option: _____

Answers 4

1   Which commands display and remove the Ruler?

    Open the *View* menu.
    Select *Ruler*.

2   When working with Word, you want to know which control keys are currently activated and also the exact position of the insertion point. Which option in the Options dialog window must be activated?

    Tab sheet: *View*
    Section: *Window*
    Option: *Status Bar*

3   Which options in the Nonprinting Characters section in the View tab sheet in the Options dialog window are advisable for normal word processing? Place a cross next to the appropriate options:

    ☒ Tab Characters
    ☐ Spaces
    ☒ Paragraph Marks
    ☒ Optional Hyphens
    ☒ Hidden Text
    ☐ All

4   Which options should be active in order to safeguard the documents as much as possible?

    Menu: *Tools*
    Command: *Options*
    Tab sheet: *Save*
    Option: *Always Create Backup Copy*
    Option: *Automatic Save Every 10 Minutes*

5 The first text

5.1 Typing the text

Example

Type the following text, exactly as it is shown in the figure. The mistakes are deliberate so that we can illustrate how they can be rectified. Keep in mind:

- When using a word processor, you do not need to do anything special to move the cursor to the beginning of the next line when a line is full. The word processor does this automatically.
- A paragraph is concluded by pressing Enter.

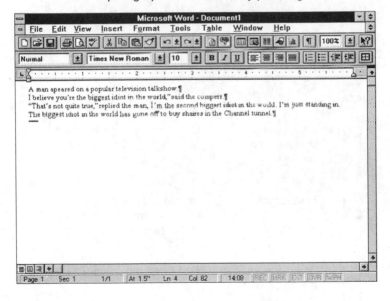

```
A man apeared on a popular television talkshow.
"I believe you're the biggest idiot in the world,"
said the comperr.
"That's not quite true," replied the man, "I'm the
```

```
second biggest idiot in the world. I'm just standing
in. The biggest idiot in the world has gone off to
buy shaires in the Channel tunnel."
```

5.2   Correcting errors

Errors which you notice while typing the text can be
rectified straightaway. We shall illustrate this using the
example text. Just ensure that the insertion point is immediately in front of or behind the character to be altered. This can be done quickly using the mouse or the
cursor keys on the keyboard. With more lengthy texts,
you can browse quickly using the scroll bar and the
corresponding arrows.

Scroll Bar, scroll arrow, scroll block	Function
Arrow Up	One line upwards
Bar between Up Arrow and scroll block	One screen page upwards
Scroll block	Indicates the relative position of the text. Dragging the block shifts the currently active text position.
Bar between Arrow Down and scroll block	One screen page downwards
Arrow Down	One line downwards

You can use the following keys and key combinations to move the insertion point (when the WordPerfect settings have been deactivated - *Tools, Options, General Tab sheet*):

Key (combination)	Function
Cursor Right	Next character
Cursor Left	Previous character
Cursor Up	One line upwards
Cursor Down	One line downwards
Home	To just in front of the first character on the line
End	Behind the last character on the line
Ctrl-PgUp	Just in front of the first character on top text line on screen
Ctrl-PgDn	Behind the last character on the bottom text line on screen
PgUp	To the previous screen page
PgDn	To the next screen page
Ctrl-Cursor Right	Just in front of the first character of the next word
Ctrl-Cursor Left	Just in front of the first character of the current word or previous word
Ctrl-Cursor Up	Just in front of the first character of the current paragraph or previous paragraph
Ctrl-Cursor Down	Just in front of the first character of the next paragraph
Ctrl-Home	Just in front of the first character of the text
Ctrl-End	Behind the last character of the text

Exercise
Correct the mistakes in the text.

```
A man apeared on a popular television talkshow.
"I believe you're the biggest idiot in the world,"
said the comperr.
"That's not quite true," replied the man, "I'm the
second biggest idiot in the world. I'm just standing
in. The biggest idiot in the world has gone off to
buy shaires in the Channel tunnel."
```

Error 1   In the first line there is the word 'apeared'.
            This should of course be 'appeared'. Move
            the insertion point to behind the **a** or the **p**
            and type the missing **p**. Normally Word is set
            to the *insert mode* which means that you can
            insert letters in the text without the existing
            letters being removed. They are just shifted
            up.

Error 2   The word 'comperr' in the second line should
            be 'compere'. Move the insertion point to just
            in front of the second **r** and press the **Ins**
            key. Word switches to the *overtype mode*.
            The letters OVR appear on the status bar.

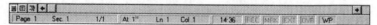

            You can now type the correct letter without
            any problems. The **e** simply replaces the **r**.
            Press the Ins key again to restore the insert
            mode. You can also switch off the overtype
            mode by double clicking on the letters OVR
            in the status bar.

Note: If the 'Use the INS key for Paste' option is
            activated in the Edit tab sheet in the Options
            dialog window, you will not be able to use
            the Ins key to switch to the overtype mode.
            In that case, you will have to activate the
            Overtype Mode option.

Error 3   The last line contains 'shaires' instead of 'shares'. You can correct this mistake in two ways:

1   Place the insertion point behind the **i** and press the **Backspace** key. This key is very useful for making corrections just after you have made the typing error.
Tip: Press Ctrl-Backspace to remove a whole word.
2   Place the insertion point just in front of the **i** and press the **Del** key. The **i** is removed and the other letters shift one position to the left.

5.3   Undoing your actions

If you are busy making corrections and you make another error, you can undo your last action:

■   Open the *Edit* menu.
■   Choose the *Undo* option.

You can also perform this action by pressing the shortcut key combinations Alt-Backspace or Ctrl-Z. This is often more convenient.

There are two buttons on the Standard toolbar which enable you to undo actions. Clicking on the left button undoes the actions, the right button reconfirms the original Undo instructions.
In this process, the Undo command is not restricted to only the last action; it applies to a large number of actions which have been carried out. If you click on the arrow next to the left button, the previous actions are listed in chronological order in an options list, with the last action at the top. You can undo a number of actions simultaneously. However, it is not possible to se-

lect separate actions from the list. For instance, if you want to undo the fourth action in the list and you select it, the three subsequent actions are also undone. The right button also has the same kind of list with previously executed actions.

Be careful when undoing several actions since it is also possible to unintentionally undo desired alterations.

5.4   Saving the text

When the text is completed, it will have to be saved otherwise you will lose it when you switch off the computer. The best thing to do is to save similar texts and documents in their own directories. For instance, you can create a directory called LETTERS where you can store your correspondence, or one called INVOICE for your financial transactions or whatever. This makes it much easier to find your documents again when you want to retrieve them.

In this book we shall presume that you save your texts on a diskette in drive A: but of course you may create your own directory as a subdirectory of WINWORD on the harddisk. To save a document proceed as follows:

- Open the *File* menu.
- Choose the *Save* option.

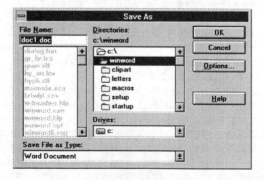

A dialog window appears. The insertion point is flashing in the File Name text box. The contents of the currently active directory are shown in the list under this text box. The file is to be stored on the diskette in drive A:. Ensure that a diskette has been inserted and proceed as follows:

- Click on the arrow next to Drive, or press Tab until the Drive section is activated. Then press the spacebar. A list of drive options is opened.
- Choose drive A: by pressing the Cursor Down key and then Enter.
- Activate the File Name text box by pressing Tab until it it activated or by clicking with the mouse.
- Type a name, for instance TV_ITEM.DOC.
- Press Enter or click on OK.

You can also open the list of drives by pressing Alt-V or by clicking on it with the mouse. You can also simply type the drive letter along with the file name in the File Name text box: *a:\tv_item.doc*. The Directories list shows the directories available in the current drive. Because Word has been started from the WINWORD directory, this directory is initially the currently active directory. Its subdirectories are shown underneath. You can select a different directory using the mouse or the keyboard.

When specifying the name, it is advisable to choose a name which gives an indication of the file contents. If you have several documents with similar contents, you can call them LETTER1, LETTER2 etc. Some characters, such as &, *, % are not allowed in file names. Word will ignore the name and the Save command until you type a valid name. The first part of the name, the part before the point, consists of a maximum of eight characters. You need not specify an extension. Word will automatically add the .DOC extension to normal documents. This is added when you have selected the Word document standard option. The Save File as Type list contains options for saving the text for use in other word processors or spreadsheets and integrated packages. Adopt the default option if you are going to continue with the text in Word.

The first time you save a file, you should open the Options dialog window by clicking on the Options button in the Save As dialog window.

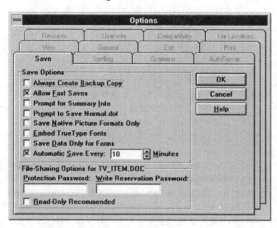

The Save tab sheet is automatically activated so that you can specify options which apply to saving files. In addition, this tab sheet provides options which you may only occasionally require. Here is a list of some of the more important options and their significance:

Always Create Backup Copy
When you save a new version of a file, a copy of the original file is created with the extension .BAK. If you unintentionally make too many errors in the new version, you can always fall back on the previous version.

Allow Fast Saves
This option is only important if the texts with which you are working are rather lengthy. Word expedites the saving process by only saving the alterations.

Note: You can only activate one of these two options. If you activate Allow Fast Saves, it is
no longer possible to make automatic back-
ups.

Prompt for Summary Info
When this option is active, a dialog window with text
boxes appears when a file is saved.

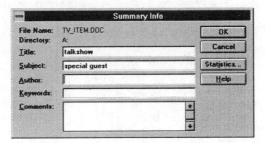

You only need to make use of this option if you create
many documents. The additional information makes it
easier to search through a great number of files for a
particular document.

Automatic Save Every *xx* Minutes
Specify the number of minutes an automatic backup is
to be made. This will restrict any loss if anything should
go wrong with your computer or the power supply.
While you are working on a text, it is only stored in
working memory. Unless your work is also saved on
disk, it will be lost as soon as the working memory is
switched off or cuts out. If the Automatic Save option is
active, the file is regularly saved to disk at the specified
interval. If a power cut or a system failure does occur,
the text which was last edited is automatically loaded
the next time the program is started up. An interval of 5
or 10 minutes is advisable, depending on your work
rate.

This tab sheet also contains options dealing with document security. The Password options enable you to

prevent other users opening your documents. The password is entered in a concealed way, in which the word itself is not shown on the screen. You have to confirm it again immediately to avoid future errors. Once this has been done, a document can only be opened when the correct password has been given.

The Write Reservation Password enables a user who does not know the password to open the document but not to save it under the same name. Thus, only users who know the correct password can make changes to the document. Others can use it and save it under a different name if they want.

The third option, Read-Only Recommended, enables you to specify that users can open the document for reading purposes only.

These options can be very useful if you are dealing with confidential or sensitive information and when you sharing a computer or are working in a network.

 When you save a text, continue to edit it and then choose the *Save* option from the *File* menu, the text is saved under the same name without any warning. If you want to assign a different name to the text, select the *Save As* option instead. You can specify a different file name in the Save As dialog window and also a different drive and directory name if required. The Save button on the Standard toolbar (the diskette, third from the left) enables you to save the file quickly and easily. Click on the button and the current text is saved under the existing file name. If the text has no name as yet, the Save As dialog window appears.

Exercise 5a

1 Everyone makes typing mistakes. Which facilities
does Word provide to rectify these and which keys
are necessary?

a _____
_____

b _____
_____

c _____
_____

2 In a momentary lapse of concentration, you replaced the words 'fair journalism' with 'hypocritical,
scandal-seeking gossip press'. What is the easiest
way to rectify this mistake?

_____
_____

3a You have created a text which is to be saved as
TEXT1 on a diskette in drive A:. Write down the
commands needed for this.

_____
_____
_____
_____
_____
_____

b You have made alterations to the text of
TEXT1.DOC and you want to save the new text
without writing over the old one. Write down the
commands needed for this.

_____
_____
_____

c   You have altered the text of TEXT1.DOC and have
    saved it using the *Save* command from the *File*
    menu. Is it still possible to work with the old ver-
    sion of TEXT1.DOC?

_____

_____

4   Type the text below. Do not enter any hyphens.
    Correct any mistakes and save the text under the
    name IMPACT.DOC.

Scientists busy investigating the effects of the impact of the Levy-Shoemaker comet on Jupiter have
made a discovery which will rock the foundation of
scientific development itself. Random photographs
indicated that there appeared to be some kind of artifacts on the dark side of our own moon. Closer in-
spection has produced the astounding theory that
these might be relics of Viking ships, although
there has been no official announcement as yet.
Some scientists have speculated that these ships
closely resemble those built in Odense, Denmark in
the seventh century. Mr. Snorre Snorregaard, curator
of the maritime museum in Odense, who happens to be
a direct descendant of Erik the Noorman, reacted
quite laconically.
"The old sagas repeatedly mention the Rainbow Bridge
which was the link to the heavens. There may be more
to these myths than we imagine."
The British Minister of Transport, Mr Brian Ma-
thingy, has demanded immediate research into the DNA
of the inhabitants of the region in that period.
"We can perhaps discover what kind of radioactive
energy was available at that time," the Minister
said. "If we could apply that today, it would be a
godsend. I mean, it takes well over an hour to get
from my country residence to my office every morning."
The Minister excused himself, saying he had to see
his bank about selling tunnel shares.

Answers 5a

1   Everyone makes typing mistakes. Which facilities does Word provide to rectify these and which keys are necessary?

      a *You can insert text by placing the insertion point at the required position using the cursor keys and key combinations.*
      b *You can type over existing text by pressing the Ins key to activate the overtype mode.*
      c *You can delete existing text by pressing Del and Backspace.*

2   In a momentary lapse of concentration, you re-placed the words 'fair journalism' with 'hypocritical, scandal-seeking gossip press'. What is the easiest way to rectify this mistake?

    Open the Edit menu and select the Undo option, or press Alt-Backspace or Ctrl-Z, or click on the Undo button.

3a   You have created a text which is to be saved as TEXT1 on a diskette in drive A:. Write down the commands needed for this.

    Open the File menu and select Save. Then select drive A: and type TEXT1 in the File Name text box. Press Enter or click on OK.

    b You have made alterations to the text of TEXT1.DOC and you want to save the new text without writing over the old one. Write down the commands needed for this.

    Open the File menu. Select Save As. Select drive A: and type the name TEXT2 in the File Name text box. Press Enter or click on OK.

    c You have altered the text of TEXT1.DOC and have saved it using the *Save* command from the *File* menu. Is it still possible to work with the old version of TEXT1.DOC?

No. Word saves the file under the same name unless you select the Save As command from the File menu.

4   Type the text below. Do not enter any hyphens. Correct any mistakes and save the text under the name IMPACT.DOC.

Hopefully, everything has gone smoothly. Save the text on diskette; you will need it later.

5.5   Switching to the Program Manager

When working under Windows, you regularly have to switch over to the Program Manager. Under Windows, it is possible to start several programs, one of which can be active at any given time. You can switch over to the other programs by means of the Task List or by pressing Alt-Tab.

Imagine that you want to save a text on a specific diskette but Word states that there is too little space available on the diskette. In that case, you have to format a new diskette; but you do not wish to close Word because that will mean that you will lose your text. What should you do?
Switch to the Program Manager via the Task List, start up the File Manager and format the new diskette. The whole procedure is as follows:

■   Open the Control menu at the left-hand side of the title bar by clicking on it or by pressing Alt-Space-bar.
■   Select *Switch To...* The Task List window appears.

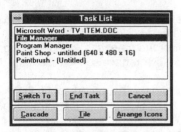

- Click on Program Manager and then on the Switch To button, or use the cursor keys and press Enter.
- Activate the File Manager by double clicking on the appropriate icon.

    If the File Manager is already shown in the Task List window, as shown here, click on it instead of on the Program Manager. Then click on the Switch To button.

- Open the *Disk* menu of the File Manager.

- Select the *Format Disk* command. The Format Disk dialog window appears.

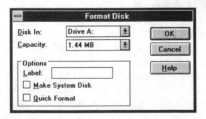

- Type the appropriate drive and disk capacity and press Enter or click on OK.
- Confirm the safeguard question or cancel the procedure if you have second thoughts.

Windows shows the progress of the formatting process. You can discontinue the formatting process if required. When the formatting has taken place, you will be asked if you want to format more diskettes. It might not be a bad idea to format several diskettes in one session to avoid a similar situation arising again in the near future.

You can return to Word in three ways. You can close the File Manager by selecting *Exit* from the *File* menu, or you can select the *Switch To...* command from the Control menu again and activate Word. The easiest method is to press Alt and hold it down. Press Tab a number of times until Word appears in a box on the screen; then release the keys.

This method of switching can be used to switch to other active programs which run under Windows, such as a spreadsheet program or a database. ,

5.6   Closing a document

When you have saved one text and wish to begin on another, you can remove the first text from working memory. The memory is now free for the next document. Proceed as follows:

- Open the *File* menu.
- Select the *Close* command.

You can also begin a new text without first closing the previous one. It is possible to have several documents open in Word at the same time.
A new empty document is opened as follows:

- Open the *File* menu.
- Select the *New* command.

The New dialog window appears containing the various templates which you can use as the basic layout for the new text. You can choose either the standard Document option or the Template option.

Word provides a number of templates which have been designed for specific aims. One of these is the Normal template in which, for instance, the margins are fixed. There are also ready-made templates for letters, memos, invoices, reports etc. Once you have become familiar with Word, you can even design your own templates and add them to this list of available templates. In the meantime, we shall work with the Normal template.

You can also open a new file by clicking on the first button at the left-hand side of the Standard toolbar. In that case, a new document is opened with the Normal template as the basic layout.

5.7   Opening a document

In the previous section you loaded a new document. This resulted in an almost empty screen with the title 'Document'. However, you will often want to retrieve a document from diskette. This cannot be done using the *New* command; it is done by selecting the *Open* command from the *File* menu.

For practice, we shall open the TV_ITEM.DOC file. Word makes it very easy for you if you have saved the document not too long ago. At the bottom of the *File* menu, Word lists the last four files with which you have worked. You can increase this number to 9 if you like, by changing the settings in the General tab sheet in the Options (*Tools, Options*) dialog window.
Open the *File* menu, insert the diskette in drive A: and select the name TV_ITEM.DOC, or type the number shown in front of the file.

File	
New...	Ctrl+N
Open...	Ctrl+O
Close	
Save	Ctrl+S
Save As...	
Save All	
Find File...	
Summary Info...	
Templates...	
Page Setup...	
Print Preview	
Print...	Ctrl+P
1 TV_ITEM.DOC	
2 TEXT1.DOC	
3 IMPACT.DOC	
Exit	

The text is displayed on the screen. You can also open an existing text by clicking on the button second from the left on the Standard toolbar. When you have done so, the Open dialog window appears.

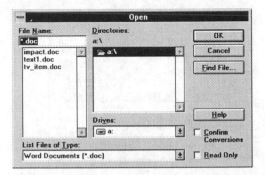

Normally Word shows here all the files with the Word extension .DOC which are stored on the drive where the previous file was saved. If you gave your file a different extension, open the List File of Type box (click on the arrow or press the Tab key to go there and then press the spacebar) and choose the appropriate extension. If you specify *.*, all the files in the currently active directory will be shown.

5.8 Printing a document

Prior to printing your document, a printer has to be installed under Windows. Printers differ in the way in which they deal with commands from the computer and, accordingly, they all have their own operating programs, called *printer drivers*. These are programs which translate the instructions from the computer. The required printer drivers for almost all printers on the market are supplied along with the Windows package.

If you installed Windows using the Setup program, the standard printer will be available for all programs which you are running under Windows. Check this by selecting the *Print* option from the *File* menu. The Print dialog window appears.

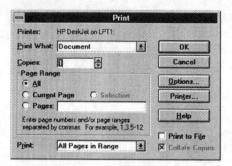

The dialog window will show which printer, if any, has been connected. You can also install another printer driver if you wish by means of the Printer button.

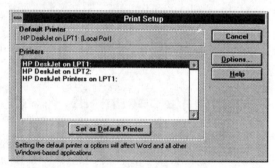

The Printer Settings dialog window displays all the printer drivers available under Windows. If required you can select a different driver and install another printer as the standard printer. In that case, the Cancel button changes into the Close button. Activating one of these buttons will return you to the Print window. If you now activate the OK button, the text will be printed on the (newly) installed standard printer.

If you are satisfied with the settings, print the text as follows:

■ Open the *File* menu.
■ Select the *Print* command.
■ Press Enter or click on OK.

If you want to print the entire document without any further ado, click on the Print button on the Standard toolbar (4th from the left). Then the Print dialog window is skipped and the printing process starts immediately.

You have now dealt with creating text, rectifying errors, saving, retrieving and printing the text. It is now time to close down the program.

5.9   Closing down Word

When you have completed working on the document and have saved it on disk, you cannot just switch off the computer. You have to close down Word in an orderly way. This is done by pressing the key combination Alt-F4, or give the following commands:

■ Open the *File* menu.
■ Select *Exit*.

If there is still a text in working memory which has not been saved in its present form, the following message box will appear:

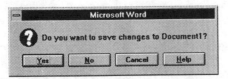

If you answer Yes to the question, Word will first save the document and then it will be closed down. If the text has no name as yet, the Save As dialog window will appear, so that you can specify a name and a path (directory and drive) for the file.

Exercise 5b

1   You are working in Word and you want to save a text but the diskette is full. Therefore you want to format a new 1.44 Mb diskette in drive A:. How do you switch to the Windows Program Manager?

_____
_____
_____
_____

Jot down the commands required to format the diskette.

_____
_____
_____
_____
_____
_____

2   What happens when you give the following instructions in succession?

open the *File* menu
select the *Close* command
open the *File* menu
select the *New* command

What do you have to specify before you can begin working on a new document?

_____

3   Which commands are needed to load the IM-
    PACT.DOC file from the diskette in drive A:?

    _____

    _____

    _____

    _____

4   Printing is no trouble if the printer has been cor-
    rectly installed. Place a cross next to the correct
    statements:

    To install a printer a printer driver is neces-
    sary.   ☐
    The installation takes place in Word by
    means of the *Print* command in the *File*
    menu.   ☐
    The printer driver has to be installed separ-
    ately for each Windows application.   ☐
    The printer is installed using the Setup in-
    stallation program from Windows so that all
    Windows applications can make use of it.   ☐

5   Which commands are given to close down Word?

    _____

    _____

6   Type the text shown below. Correct any typing er-
    rors and save the text on your work diskette under
    the name PRINTER.DOC.

Printer types and capacity

Anyone who is thinking of buying a printer should
have a good look around before doing so in order to
avoid disappointment and frustration later. Here is
a list of the types of printers currently available
on the market:

I Impact printers

Impact printers are printers which place the text on paper by means of pushing the character against the ink ribbon and on to the paper.

1 Line printers

This is the oldest type of printer, now considered unsuitable for use in the office or study. These have an enormous capacity, but the type and size of the letters are fixed. As the name indicates, they print a whole line in one go by means of placing the letters on a cylinder, chain or rod.

2 Daisywheel printers

The text is printed character by character using a daisy wheel. The characters are situated on a disk which turns making each character available. These are in fact printers which have their origin in the electric typewriter. They can reproduce various fonts and font sizes because the wheel with the letters can be replaced. The printing quality is excellent. However, daisy wheel printers cannot print graphic images.

3 Matrix printers

These were the cheapest and accordingly the most popular printers in combination with the PC. With matrix printers the letters are formed by a collection of points. Each point is placed on the paper by pressing a pin against the ink ribbon and on to the paper. The more pins there are the better the print quality. Matrix printers can reproduce many different fonts, such as:

Arial 8 pts dark green
Courier New 12 pts ochre
Times New Roman 16 pts red
Wingdings 20 pts blue

II Non-impact printers

Non-impact printers are printers where the print head does not come into direct contact with the paper.

4 Inkjet printers
Inkjet printers are becoming increasingly less ex-
pensive and are beginning to form a threat to the
leading market position of the matrix printers. Inkjet printers spray the ink through tiny jets on to
the paper. The great advantage of this method is
that it takes places almost silently. Only the action of moving the paper and the ink cartridge make
any noise. The print quality is excellent.

5 Laser printers
These printers produce the best quality print. The
characters are burnt into the paper by means of the
same method as photocopy machines also use. Laser
printers are faster than inkjet printers and give
even better quality. They also work almost silently.

Answers 5b

1   You are working in Word and you want to save a
    text but the diskette is full. Therefore you want to
    format a new 1.44 Mb diskette in drive A:. How do
    you switch to the Windows Program Manager?

    Open the Control menu on the title bar.
    Select Switch To...
    Select Program Manager.
    Press Enter or click on Switch To.

    Jot down the commands required to format the
    diskette.

    Switch to the File Manager.
    Open the Disk menu.
    Select the Format Disk command.
    Specify the appropriate drive and capacity.
    Press Enter or click on OK.
    Answer Yes to the safeguard question.

2   What happens when you give the following instructions in succession?

open the *File* menu
select the *Close* command
open the *File* menu
select the *New* command

The document which is currently in working memory is closed and stored on disk if required. A new empty document is opened.

What do you have to specify before you can begin working on a new document?

Prior to beginning work you have to specify whether you want to create a document or a template. If you want to create a document, you still have to specify which type of template you wish to use (this will be NORMAL for normal texts).

3   Which commands are needed to load the IM-PACT.DOC file from the diskette in drive A:?

Open the File menu.
Select Open.
Select the appropriate drive.
Select IMPACT.DOC.
Click on OK or press Enter.

4   Printing is no trouble if the printer has been correctly installed. Place a cross next to the correct statements:

To install a printer a printer driver is necessary.   ☒

The installation takes place in Word by means of the *Print* command in the *File*   ☐
menu.

The printer driver has to be installed separately for each Windows application.   ☐

The printer is installed using the Setup installation program from Windows so that all Windows applications can make use of it. ⊠

5   Which commands are given to close down Word?

Open the File menu.
Select the Exit command.

6   Compare your text to the example. Use the information given in this chapter to solve any problems that might arise.

6   Improving your text

6.1   Spelling check

Even the most experienced writer makes typing errors.
Word makes it possible to check your texts for spelling
mistakes. To do this, select the *Speller* option from the
Tools menu. When you have done this, the
Spelling:English dialog window appears.

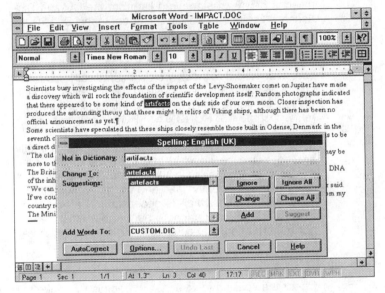

The words in your text are compared to the words in
the Word dictionary. If the Speller encounters a word
which is not in the dictionary, the Spelling dialog window is displayed in the Not in Dictionary text box. In
many cases, Word will suggest an alternative for the
word in question.

In our IMPACT example text, the word 'artifacts' is
spelled incorrectly. The proper suggestion is made in
the Suggestions box. Accept this suggestion by clicking

on the Change button or by pressing Alt-C. The text is immediately altered and the spelling check moves on to the next word.

The next word at which the spelling check stops is 'Odense'. We know that this is correctly spelled, but because it does not occur in the Word dictionary, Word presumes it to be incorrect and makes other proposals. If you like, you can add this word to your own Custom dictionary by activating the Add button. Later you can select a newly created word list from the Custom Dictionaries list in the Spelling tab sheet in the Options dialog window. All the words which do not occur in the standard Word dictionary can be adopted into lists like these. This type of list is then available for all texts. If you wish to order these words thematically, you can create various adapted Custom Dictionaries. Assign these a file name which gives an indication of their contents, such as ASTRONOM or SPORT for instance.

In our text, the word 'Odense', which is correctly spelled, could be adopted into this type of list. However, we do not wish to include it in a custom list since it will not be frequently used and we do not wish to occupy more memory than is necessary. The best thing to do is to click on the Ignore button. If a word were to occur more often, you could also click on the Ignore All button.

Example
Check the spelling in your text. If necessary, make the required changes. Save the corrected text under the name IMPACT.DOC.

6.2 Deleting, moving and copying text

In order to be able to delete, insert and move text, the corresponding passages of text must first be selected (also referred to as *marked*).

Selecting passages of text

You can select passages of text using both the mouse
and the keyboard. You must first place the insertion
point at the beginning of the relevant section of text. If
you are using the keyboard, press **F8** and then the cursor keys, or press the Shift key and the cursor keys.
The various keystrokes and key combinations for selecting text are listed below:

Key(s)	Function
F8	Activates the selection; EXT is shown on the status line.
Two x F8	Selects the word before, behind or in which the insertion point is situated.
Three x F8	Selects the sentence before, behind or in which the insertion point is situated.
Four x F8	Selects the current paragraph.
Five x F8	Selects the entire text.
Shift	Hold down the Shift key and use the cursor keys to select the required sections. Special combinations are:
Shift-Ctrl-Cursor Right	Selects the next word.
Shift-Ctrl-Cursor Left	Selects the previous word.
Shift-Home	Selects from the insertion point to the beginning of the line.
Shift-End	Selects from the insertion point to the end of the line.
Shift-Ctrl-Cursor Up	Selects one paragraph from the insertion point upwards.
Shift-Ctrl-Cursor Down	Selects one paragraph from the insertion point downwards.

Shift-Ctrl-PgUp	Selects from the insertion point to the first character on the screen.
Shift-Ctrl-PgDn	Selects from the insertion point to the last character on the screen.
Shift-PgUp	Selects the previous screen page from the insertion point backwards.
Shift-PgDn	Selects the next screen page from the insertion point onwards.
Shift-Ctrl-Home	Selects the text from the insertion point to the beginning of the text.
Shift-Ctrl-End	Selects the text from the insertion point to the end of the text.

You can also select any section of text using the mouse. To do this, place the mouse pointer in front of the first character of the required text. Hold down the left mouse button and drag the mouse to the end of the passage to be selected. Keep the following details in mind:

Action	Result
Double click on a word	Selects the word.
Click in the selection area	Selects the adjacent line.
Hold down Ctrl and click in a sentence	Selects the sentence.
Double click in the selection area	Selects the adjacent paragraph.
Hold down Ctrl and click in the selection area	Selects the entire text.

Note: A selection is undone by pressing one of the cursor keys unless you have selected text by means of the F8 function key. This type of selection is undone by first pressing Esc to neutralize the effects of F8 and then pressing one of the cursor keys.

Deleting text

Prior to being able to delete text, it must first be selected. You can remove separate characters using Backspace or Delete without having to select them first.

Example
Load the IMPACT text from the work diskette and remove the second paragraph. To do this, proceed as follows:

- Select the appropriate paragraph.
- Press Del.

A text which you delete in this way is in principle irretrievably lost. But with most activities in Word you are given a chance to undo the last action.

Example
Undo the deletion of the paragraph (see also chapter 5).

- Open the *Edit* menu.
- Select *Undo Clear*.

Moving sections of text

Word provides two methods of moving sections of text:

- Moving sections of text without making use of the Clipboard (dragging and dropping);
- Moving sections via the Clipboard.

Example
Type the following text.

```
The Rules .

Past, present and future

The inclination to kick a stone is as old as the ex-
istence of the shoe. In almost all cultures, games
```

have come into being in which people played an object with their feet, frequently in combination with hands and/or sticks.

There are also ancient stories (the Aztecs, the Vikings) about warfare in which the victors used their feet to roll the severed heads of the vanquished in an orgy of triumph.

Early official documents mention ball games in north-west France in the 13th and 14th century. Various (football) games were played in Great Britain in the 15th century, King James I of Scotland actually forbidding football by decree because of the unruly character of the game and because it withheld the men from practising archery. Brailsford describes a typical scene:
"Heads and legs were broken and deaths were not unusual as the sides pushed, hacked and kicked their ways through streets of shuttered shops, through streams of mud, waste land and fallow."

Almost all ball games have a common concept as their ancestor. A ball or ball-like object has to be brought through the opponents' lines with the aim of placing it in a particular place. Think of modern games of rugby, American football, hockey, handball, basketball etc.

Soccer historians think of the 1st of December 1863 as being the birth date of the modern version of the game. On that day, separate rules were formulated for soccer (association football) and rugby. But it took until 1869 before field players in soccer were forbidden to play the ball with their hands or arms. This was a major change and is still the most important rule in soccer today.

With all due respect to other sports which call themselves 'football', soccer is the only real foot sport. Except when the goalkeeper has caught it, the ball is always free. The fact that the ball is al-

ways accessible to all players is the mainspring of
the game.

(From *Soccer For Dummies* by Hall, Kuilman and
vanBatenburg)

We shall now move the second paragraph ('There
are..'), joining it to the first ('The inclination..).

When you want to move text without making use of the
Clipboard, the Drag and Drop option on the Edit tab
sheet in the Options dialog window has to be active. If
you use the keyboard, the procedure is as follows:

■ Select the paragraph including the paragraph
   marking (double click in the selection area or
   4xF8).
■ Press F2. The status bar displays the question
   'Move to where?'.
■ Specify the destination by placing the broken insertion point in front of the required position using
   the cursor keys.
■ Press Enter.

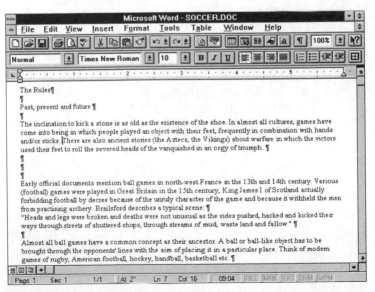

If you are working with the mouse, place the mouse pointer in the selected section of text, press the left mouse button and hold it down. A rectangle appears under the mouse pointer and a dotted insertion point is displayed at the arrowhead. Place this dotted insertion point at the position where the text is to be inserted. As soon as you release the mouse button, the section of text is moved to the specified position.

Remove the two empty lines and save the text on the work diskette under the name SOCCER.

If you wish to move a section of text via the Clipboard, this is done by marking it first, cutting it out and inserting it at the required position.

Example
We shall close the currently active document and load the PRINTER.DOC document once more. We shall now move the heading 'Printer types and capacity' to the blank line between the first paragraph and the subheading 'Impact printers'. This time we shall make use of the Clipboard.

Proceed as follows:

- Select the heading including the paragraph marking.
- Open the *Edit* menu.
- Choose the *Cut* command.
- Specify the position where the text is to be placed by moving the insertion point to it.
- Open the *Edit* menu.
- Choose the *Paste* command.

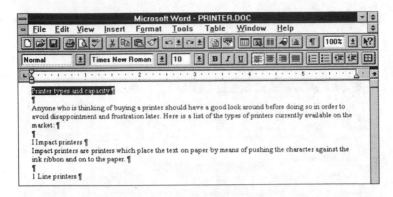

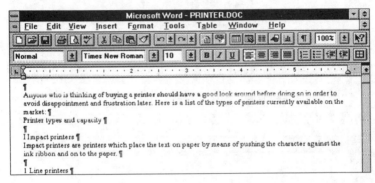

Instead of using the *Cut* command from the *Edit* menu, you can also use the key combination Ctrl-X or Shift-Del. You can also click on the Cut button (the button with the scissors) on the Standard toolbar. And instead of the *Paste* command from the *Edit* menu, you can also press the key combination Ctrl-V or Shift-Ins. You

can also use the Paste button (the ninth button) on the Standard toolbar.

The right-hand mouse button activates the shortcut menu

If you wish to carry out certain actions with a passage of text, select the passage first. Commands for editing the text are to be found in the menus. In addition, many frequently-used commands have been placed in a so-called *shortcut* menu. This shortcut menu is activated by pressing the right mouse button.

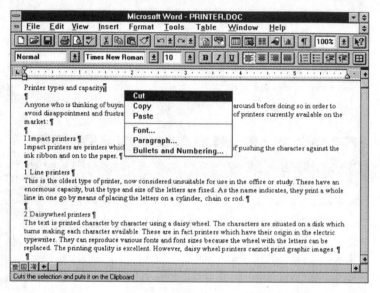

In this way, you can, for example, cut and paste a paragraph elsewhere without having to move to a menu on the menu bar.

The Clipboard

If you wish to examine the contents of the Clipboard, switch to the Program Manager. The Clipboard Viewer application is situated in the Main group window. Double click on the application icon to open the Clipboard.

Copying text

When text is copied, it remains at the original position and is also inserted at another position. The method used for this is similar to that used in the moving procedure.

Example
Just for practice we shall copy the heading in our PRINTER article to the end of the text.

You do not need to make use of the Clipboard when copying. You can simply use the *drag and drop* method.
If you are using the keyboard, press the key combination Shift-F2. If you are using the mouse, place the mouse pointer in the selected text. Then press Ctrl and hold it down. Press the left mouse button and hold it down too. Drag the text to the required new position before releasing both.

If you prefer to work with the Clipboard, select the *Copy* command from the *Edit* menu, or press Ctrl-C. The text is then copied to the Clipboard. Then move the insertion point to the required position and choose the *Paste* command from the *Edit* menu, or press Ctrl-V or Shift-Ins.
The Standard toolbar provides the Copy (next to Cut) and the Paste (next to Copy) buttons.

Example
Use the currently active document to practise moving and copying sections of text. Close the document without saving it.

Exercise 6a

1   Which keys or key combinations are used to select
    the following sections of text?

    A word _____
    A sentence _____
    The entire text _____
    From the insertion point to
    the end of the line _____
    Paragraphs downwards from
    the insertion point _____
    From the insertion point to
    the end of the text _____

2   A paragraph is to be moved to the end of the text.
    Which facilities does Word provide for doing this?

    _____
    _____
    _____
    _____

Answers 6a

1   Which keys or key combinations are used to select
    the following sections of text?

A word	*Press F8 twice*
A sentence	*Press F8 three times*
The entire text	*Press F8 five times*
From the insertion point to the end of the line	*Shift-End*
Paragraphs down-wards from the insertion point	*Shift-Ctrl-Cursor Down*
From the insertion point to the end of the text	*Shift-Ctrl-End*

2   A paragraph is to be moved to the end of the text.
    Which facilities does Word provide for doing this?

*Without using the Clipboard, you can drag and
drop the selected paragraph to the new position. If
you wish to use the Clipboard, choose the Cut
command from the Edit menu to move the selected text to the Clipboard. Move the insertion
point to the required position and choose Paste
from the Edit menu.*

6.3   Formatting characters

You can apply certain features to the characters in your
text to give it a more attractive appearance. Bold, underlining, italics and capital letters help to emphasize
passages and thus make the text more accessible and
easy to read.

You can only apply many of the possibilities if you have
a printer which can deal with graphic characters. Most
matrix, inkjet and laser printers are capable of this.

In Word, you can alter character attributes:

■   using key combinations
■   using functions from the *Format* menu
■   using the Formatting toolbar.

Key combinations for formatting characters

The following key combinations change the appearance of selected characters:

Key combination Effect

Key combination	Effect
Ctrl-Shift-Z	Standard layout, all attributes can-celled
Ctrl-B	Bold
Ctrl-I	Italics
Ctrl-Shift-K	Small capitals
Ctrl-U	Continuing underlined
Ctrl-Shift-W	Underlined per word
Ctrl-Shift-D	Double underlined
Ctrl-Shift-Equals sign	Superscript
Ctrl-Equals sign	Subscript
Ctrl-Shift-H	Hidden text
Shift-F3	Display selected text in capitals or small letters

You can also combine these key combinations so that a word, for example, can be both bold and underlined. If you wish to cancel a certain format, press the same key combination once more.

The character format displayed on your screen depends on the display mode: characters which are given the bold attribute will be shown in boldface unless you have activated the Draft Output check box in the View tab sheet in the Options dialog window.

Example
We shall load the SOCCER text and display the title in small capitals. This is done as follows when using the keyboard:

■ Press Ctrl-Home to place the insertion point in front of the title.
■ Press Shift-End or F8 three times.
■ Press Ctrl-Shift-K.

This is done as follows when using the mouse:

■ Place the mouse pointer in front of the title.
■ Press the left mouse button.
■ Press the key combination Ctrl-Shift-K.

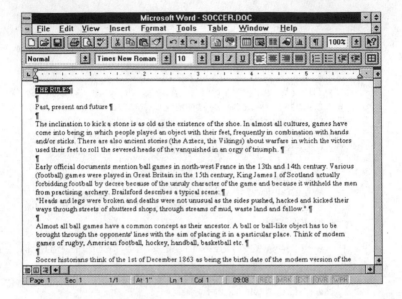

Example

We shall change the acknowledgements at the end of the article to italics. This is done as follows:

- Place the insertion point at the end of the text.
- Select the entire line.
- Press Ctrl-I or click on the Italics button on the Formatting toolbar (the button with the *I*).

The text should now look something like this:

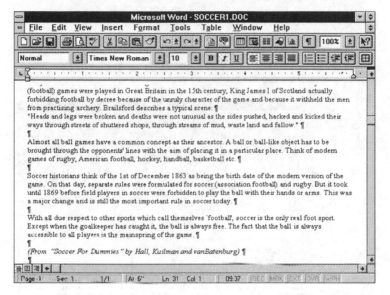

Save the text as SOCCER1.

Example
If you know that certain sections of a text are to be written in italics, you can apply the character format as you type. This is done as follows:

- Press Ctrl-I.
- Type the text. It is immediately shown in italics.
- Press Ctrl-I when you wish to return to the standard text.

Other formatting features can be applied in a similar way.

Formatting using menu commands

You can also format characters without having to learn
key combinations by heart. It is a little more time-consuming, but the *Font* option from the *Format* menu produces the same effect. When you select this option, the
Font dialog window appears:

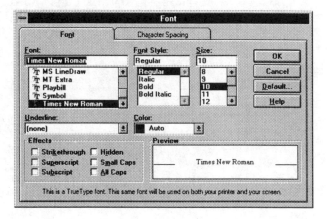

■ Open the *Format* menu.
■ Choose *Font*.
■ Choose the Font tab sheet if it is not already se-
  lected.
■ Select the required option and press Enter or click
  on OK.

In this dialog window, you can specify much more than
bold or italics attributes. You can also select the font
(the type of letter), the font size and the character spacing for a selected section of text. This dialog window
also provides facilities for displaying letters in colour.

Font and font size

The choice of font and font size also determines the
appearance of your text to a large extent. The exact

possibilities depend on the type of printer which is connected. The various fonts are listed in the Font: section in the Font dialog window.

Certain fonts in the list are preceded by the letters TT which stand for *TrueType*. TrueType fonts are fonts which are available from Windows 3.1 onwards. With these fonts, the screen display is identical to the final printout. Other fonts in the list are preceded by a printer symbol; these are the so-called *printer fonts*. The screen display may differ to the result from the printer when these are applied.

Some of the fonts are *proportional fonts*. This means that the space used to display the characters (on both the screen and on paper) is adjusted to accommodate the shape of the letter. An i for example occupies much less space than a w.

If you wish to indent a text at certain places in order to create a list for example, the non-proportional fonts are more suited to this function.

The Symbol and Wingdings fonts provide special characters which can be included in a text. We shall return to this topic shortly.

The font Size list provides various point sizes for the fonts. These depend on the selected font and the connected printer. The font size is given in points. There are 72 points to one inch.

Example
We shall give the entire text a font size of 12 points. The penultimate paragraph will be given a 16 points size.

This is done as follows:

■   Select the whole text.
■   Open the *Format* menu.

- Choose the *Font* option.
- Select the Font tab sheet if necessary.
- Select the 12 points font size.
- Press Enter or click on OK.

Now select the penultimate paragraph and allocate a 16 points font size in the same way.

The default setting in Word is the Times New Roman font and a 10 points font size. Some people may find this rather small and difficult to read. However, it is possible to define a different font and font size as the default settings. The Font tab sheet in the Font dialog window has the Default button by means of which you can specify the currently active settings as the standard settings for the Normal template. If you do so, from that moment on, the specified font and font size become the standard settings for all documents which are created by means of this template.

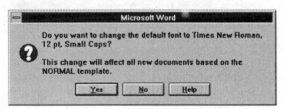

Character Spacing

Example
We shall increase the spacing in the title The Rules by 4 points.

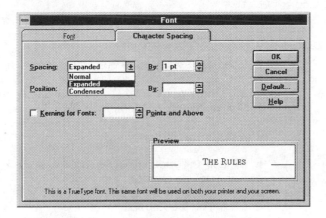

The Font dialog window contains the Character Spacing tab sheet in addition to the Font tab sheet. The options in the Character Spacing list enable you to determine whether a passage of text should be made wider or narrower. This can be done in intervals of 0.1 pt. This is particularly convenient when formatting titles. The options in the Position enable you to move passages of text in steps of 1 pt. The preview section of the dialog window displays the effects of the alterations so that you can examine these prior to confirmation using OK.

The Character Spacing option enables you to alter the distance between the characters, depending on the selected font and the characters in question. The distance will be larger with broad characters than with narrow ones.

Save the altered text under the name SOCCER2.

Character format using the Formatting toolbar

The Formatting toolbar enables you to alter the font or font size quickly and easily, and to display the text in boldface, italics or underlined.

Example
Load the Impact document.

If necessary, activate the Formatting toolbar by means of the *Toolbar* option in the *View* menu. We shall change three words in the third paragraph to italics. We shall then save the document as SHIPS.

This is done as follows:

- Place the mouse pointer on the word 'Rainbow' and double click on the word.
- Click with the mouse on the Italics button (showing the *I*) on the Formatting toolbar.
- Repeat these actions for the other words, 'Bridge' and 'myths'.

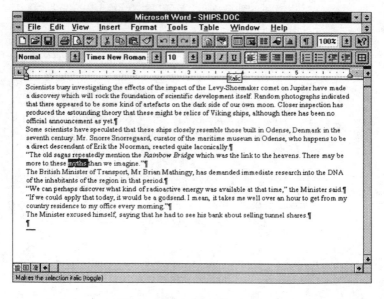

Once you have clicked on the Italics button, the word is displayed in italics. The button itself is shown in a lighter shade of grey. If you click on the button once more while the selection is still active, the character formatting is undone.

You can also use the Formatting toolbar to alter the font size. To do this, select the section of text first and then move the mouse pointer to the arrow next to the Font Size box. Click with the left mouse button to open the list of options and select the required point size from the list.

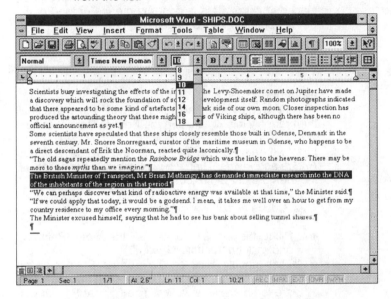

You can also activate the Font options list from the Formatting toolbar using the keyboard. This is done by pressing Ctrl-Shift-F. You can then press the Cursor Down and Cursor Up keys to move to the required font. Press Enter.

Having activated the Font options list, if you then press Tab, the Font Size options list is activated. You can also activate this list using the key combination Ctrl-Shift-P. The point size can again be selected by pressing the cursor keys and then Enter.

Copying the format

We have converted various passages of text to italics.
These procedures can be carried out more quickly and
easily by selecting one section of text and copying the
text format to other sections of text which have to be
placed in italics. This is done by means of the Format
Painter button on the Standard toolbar.

Example
We shall remove the italics in the SHIPS text. We shall
then reapply this style using the Format Painter button.

First we remove the italics on the words *Rainbow
Bridge* and *myths*. Then we shall reapply the italics using the Format Painter button.

This is done as follows:

- Place the mouse pointer on the word 'Rainbow'
  and click on the Italics button.
- Then double click on the Format Painter button
  and subsequently click on the other words which
  are to be shown in italics. The Format Painter button remains active until you press Esc or click on
  the button again. You can now copy the format to
  other required positions.
- Click on all the words to which you wish to apply
  this format. If you only click once on the Format
  Painter button, you can only copy the format once.

Save the document and close it.

Exercise 6b

1   Which keystrokes produce the following results?

Small capitals _____

Underlining _____

Superscript _____

Italics _____

2   Applying other fonts and font sizes allows you to make your texts more attractive. What are the default font and font size in Word?

_____

_____

This font has one disadvantage. Which?

_____

_____

_____

You wish to format a text and to print it in the Arial font with a font size of 12 points. Which commands have to be given?

_____

_____

_____

_____

_____

3   Which character formatting facilities are provided by the Formatting toolbar?

_____

_____

_____

_____

_____

_____

4   Load the SOCCER text and place the subheading in italics as shown in the figure below. When you have done this, the text should be assigned the Times New Roman 12 pts. font. There must be no typing errors. Save the text under the name KICK.

It should look like this:

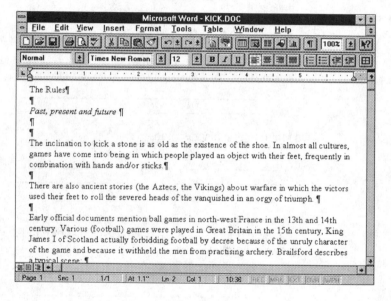

Answers 6b

1   Which keystrokes produce the following results?

Small capitals   *Ctrl-Shift-K*
Underlining   *Ctrl-U*
Superscript   *Ctrl-Shift-Equals sign*
Italics   *Ctrl-I*

2   Applying other fonts and font sizes allows you to make your texts more attractive. What are the default font and font size in Word?

Times New Roman
Pts: 10

This font has one disadvantage. Which?

It is a proportional font, which means that the characters have different widths. If you use indentation you may get uneven edges.

You wish to format a text and to print it in the Arial font with a font size of 12 points. Which commands have to be given?

Select the entire text.
Select the Font option from the Format *menu.*
Select the Font tab sheet.
Select the Arial font and the font size 12 pts.
Click on OK.

3   Which character formatting facilities are provided by the Formatting toolbar?

Font
Font Size
Bold
Italics
Underlining

4   Load the SOCCER text and place the subheading
in italics as shown in the figure below. When you
have done this, the text should be assigned the
Times New Roman 12 pts. font. There must be no
typing errors. Save the text under the name KICK.

*Compare your results to the example shown. The
subheading is placed in italics by selecting it
(move the insertion point to the beginning of the
line and press F8 three times) and then pressing
Ctrl-I or click on the Italics button. Subsequently
select the entire text by pressing F8 or dragging
the mouse. Open the point size list by clicking on it
or pressing Ctrl-Shift-P and then Cursor down. Activate the required point size. The spelling check is
carried out by pressing the shortcut key, F7.*

6.4   Formatting paragraphs

The appearance and legibility of text are enhanced by
good character formatting. The general appearance of
the document is made more attractive by good paragraph formatting. We shall discuss this in some detail
in the following section. Just to be clear: *a paragraph is
a section of text separated from other sections of text
by a Hard Return, in other words, by pressing Enter.*

Example
Type the text shown below. Ensure that the headings
above the paragraphs are separated from the paragraphs by pressing Shift-Enter instead of Enter. This
ensures that they are regarded as being part of the paragraph. The non-printing paragraph marks should be
displayed by activating the Paragraph Marks option in
the View tab sheet in the Options dialog window. You
will see on the screen the difference between the line
wrap (Shift-Enter) and the paragraph marks (Enter).

Flying reptiles

Pterosaurs had a fine covering of hair over their bodies. Fur is a reliable indicator, and most paleontologists accept that the pterosaurs were warmblooded. This would provide the high metabolic rate that was necessary for an active flying lifestyle. There is no doubt that pterosaurs were efficient flapping fliers, although some of the later Cretaceous forms were so huge that gliding seems more likely. It has also been argued more recently that they could have run about on the ground like small dinosaurs, with their wings folded, rather than fumbling along as a grounded bat has to do.

Birds

In the case of the *Archaeopteryx*, the pigeon-sized skeleton has broadly the shape of a small therapod dinosaur's, with therapod features like a long bony tail, claws on its fingers and teeth in its jaws. But, according to most paleontologists, the possession of feathers makes *Archaeopteryx* a bird.

Feathers

The origin of feathers is a puzzle that *Archaeopteryx* does not solve, since its own are fully modern. Feathers like hairs and reptilian scales are made from the tough protein keratin, so they probably derive from a therapod dinosaur that happened to develop "ragged" scales and then retained them, probably as a form of insulation. After that, longer feathers on the forearm may have helped the wearer to leap after prey, or to escape. Most evidence suggests that *Archaeopteryx* was a tree-climber, using sets of claws on both its "hand-wing" and its toes, and that flight arose as a development from gliding, which would have enabled the proto-bird to move rapidly about the upper story of forests.

(Michael Benton)

Format the entire text in Courier New 12 pts and save it under the name FEATHERS.

You have now briefly touched on the possibilities of formatting paragraphs. The Shift-Enter key combination produces a new line but does not conclude the paragraph.

In Word, you can separate sections of text in the following ways:

Key combination	Effect
Enter	new paragraph
Shift-Enter	new line
Ctrl-Enter	new page
Ctrl-Shift-Enter	new column

We shall return to the functions for a new page and a new column shortly. In the FEATHERS text, the second and third paragraphs are to be indented. Subsequently the lines are to be fully justified so that not only the left edge but also the right edge has an even margin. We shall activate the automatic hyphenation to prevent too large spaces occurring in the words.

There are five methods of formatting paragraphs in Word:

1   using key combinations
2   using menu commands
3   using the Ruler
4   using the Formatting toolbar
5   using the Standard toolbar.

Formatting paragraphs using key combinations

When formatting paragraphs, keep in mind that the commands you give apply to the paragraph in which the insertion point is currently situated. If, as in our example, you wish to format several paragraphs in one go, you must select them first.

Word provides the following key combinations for formatting paragraphs:

Key combination Effect

Key combination	Effect
Ctrl-J	Full justification
Ctrl-L	Left-alignment
Ctrl-R	Right-alignment
Ctrl-E	Centring text
Ctrl-1	Single line spacing
Ctrl-2	Double line spacing
Ctrl-5	Line spacing at one and a half
Ctrl-0	Extra line before the paragraph
Ctrl-M	Left-indent a paragraph
Ctrl-Shift-M	Right-indent a paragraph
Ctrl-T	Increase the left indent to the next tab stop
Ctrl-Shift-T	Decrease the left indent to the previous tab stop
Ctrl-Q	Remove all direct formatting of the selected paragraph

The default tab stop setting is 0.5". This is not unimportant since it has a proportional relation to the size of the font. Certain settings may negatively influence the text alignment when indentation is applied. You should always check the tab settings when formatting.

Example
We shall check if the default tab setting is 0.5". This is done as follows:

- Open the *Format* menu.
- Select the *Tabs* option.
- Specify the tab settings at 0.5 in the Default Tab Stops text box.
- Click on OK.

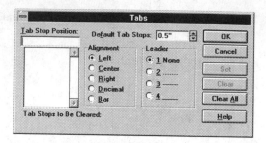

The other options in this dialog box are discussed in the section about Tabs a little further on in the book.

Example
We shall apply indentation to the second and third paragraphs.
This is done as follows:

- Select the appropriate paragraphs.
- Press Ctrl-M.

Example
We shall now justify the text.

- Select the entire text.
- Press Ctrl-J.

Unfortunately, the result is not yet something we would write home about. Because Word regards the headings above the paragraphs as being one line, they are completely stretched to fill the line. This can be altered in two ways. If you change the line wrap to a paragraph mark and then justify all paragraphs separately, you can omit the headings from the justification process. The second method is to protect the spaces in the headings. This is done by replacing all spaces with hard spaces (Ctrl-Shift-Spacebar).

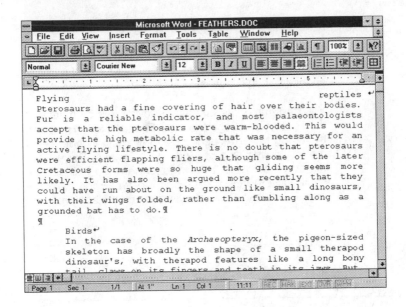

A font like Courier is not very suitable for full justification. The default font, Times New Roman, produces a much more attractive page. The best results are produced when you select this type of proportional font along with a quality printer. Any excess space on a line is divided evenly among all the characters.

Restore the normal left-alignment by pressing the key combination Ctrl-L.

Use the FEATHERS text to experiment with other formatting features. Close this text without saving it (*File, Close*). Then load the original FEATHERS text again to begin again with an unformatted text.

Formatting paragraphs using the menu bar

The text became much more legible due to the initial changes we made (Courier 12 pts). To improve it further, we shall apply options from the *Format* menu.

The subheadings above the paragraphs should not be indented; this will help emphasize them. The default paragraph indentation is too large: an indentation of two characters is sufficient. We shall make the corresponding modifications.

You can make fine alterations to the text by means of the *Paragraph* option from the *Format* menu. However, there you have to specify the settings in inches, centimetres, points or picas, not in characters. But we are not sure how wide the characters are. To find out, we shall activate the Ruler. Open the *View* menu and select *Ruler* if it is not already shown on the screen.

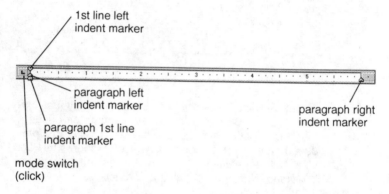

1st line left
indent marker

paragraph left
indent marker

paragraph right
indent marker

paragraph 1st line
indent marker

mode switch
(click)

The units of measurement used depend on the settings in the View tab sheet in the Options dialog box. In this book, we use the normal inches settings. The Ruler is 6 inches long, the page 8 inches wide and the left and right margins are both 1 inches wide. You may prefer to work in centimetres to conform to our European friends. Change the settings in the View tab sheet if you prefer. They will then apply to all subsequent documents.

We see that two characters occupy roughly a quarter of an inch with a font like Courier New. We wish to indent the paragraph by a quarter of an inch (excepting the headings). This is done as follows:

■ Select the paragraph.
■ Open the *Format* menu.
■ Select the *Paragraph* option.
■ Select the Indents and Spacing tab sheet if necessary.
■ Set the value in the Left: text box 0".
■ Select the Hanging option from the Special list.
■ Type 0.25 in the By: text box.
■ Press Enter or click on OK.

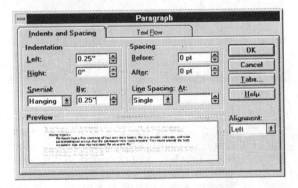

The Hanging option ensures that the paragraph is indented by the specified distance (0.25", 2 characters). The first line is excluded from this. The blocks on the Ruler indicate that the specified modifications have taken place.

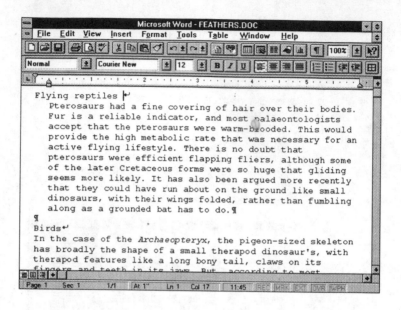

The Indents and Spacing tab sheet in the Paragraph dialog window provides more possibilities. The Alignment option list contains options for aligning sections of text either left, right or centre. A custom indentation can only be specified via the dialog window. Key combinations enable you to indent to the tab stops for which the setting here is 0.5".

In the Spacing section, you can specify a number of blank lines between the paragraphs; you can also define the line spacing of these blank lines. These blank lines replace the empty paragraphs (between the two Hard Returns) which we have used up until now in our examples.

In the Pagination section of the Text Flow tab sheet, you can determine when Word is to place text on a new page. If you wish to have page breaks after all paragraphs, activate the Page Break Before option. The end of the page is then shown on screen as a horizontal dotted line. This kind of page break can only be deactivated via this dialog window. The option Keep with Next ensures that two paragraphs are not separated by the page break. If the two paragraphs no longer fit on to the page, Word will place them both on a new page. The frequently-used option Keep Lines Together ensures that the page break does not occur in the middle of a paragraph.

The Suppress Line Numbers option ensures that line numbers in a text are not shown.

Formatting paragraphs using the Ruler

Just as with character formatting, Word provides a separate facility for formatting paragraphs using the mouse. The Ruler is the focal point here. We shall illustrate this by means of our FEATHERS text.

Example
We shall format paragraphs two and three using the mouse. Move the insertion point to the beginning of the second paragraph.

In order to be able to work with the Ruler and the mouse, it is advisable to increase the display on screen so that the movements of the mouse pointer can be seen in more detail. This is done by opening the *View* menu and selecting the *Zoom* option. In the subsequent dialog window, specify the Zoom To settings at 200%.

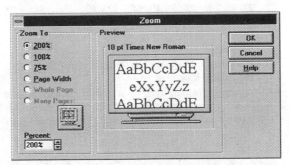

To make a left indentation, place the mouse pointer on the small triangle above the small square block in the lower left-hand part of the Ruler. Press the left mouse button. A vertical dotted line appears on the screen indicating the position of the indentation. Move the small triangle to just behind the second letter of the first word of the second paragraph (Birds). The paragraph is automatically formatted with a hanging indent equal to two characters. If you wish to indent the whole paragraph, move the block which is under the small triangle. In that case, both blocks are moved. The upper triangle allows you to specify a separate indentation later.

Format the third paragraph in the same way.

If you use the Ruler, you have the advantage that you do not need to learn the key combinations by heart. In addition, this method of working is more practical and quicker. A disadvantage is that the Ruler occupies screen space.

Now restore the screen display to 100% zoom once more via the appropriate option in the *View* menu.

Save the text under the name FEATHERS.

Formatting paragraphs using the Formatting toolbar

The Formatting toolbar enables you to apply quick paragraph formatting using the mouse. We shall illustrate this using the Feathers document.

Example
We shall justify the first paragraph and right-align the acknowledgement at the end. First replace the normal space between the two words of the heading with a fixed space by typing Ctrl-Shift-Spacebar. Now the words will be kept together. The justification is implemented as follows:

- Select the first paragraph of the text.
- Click on the Justify button on the Formatting tool-bar.

The last line can be right-aligned in a similar way:

- Select the acknowledgement at the end of the text.
- Click on the Right-align button on the Formatting toolbar.

Save the text under the name FEATHER2 and close the document.

The Formatting toolbar has two buttons which enable you to quickly apply paragraph indentation.

indent paragraph one tab stop extra

indent paragraph one tab stop less

The right-hand button of these two (Increase Indent) in-dents the paragraph by one extra tab stop; clicking on the left-hand button (Decrease Indent) will undo this.

Example
We shall load the FEATHER2 text and select the first paragraph. This will be indented by two standard tab stops.

To do this, select the relevant paragraph and click twice on the Increase Indent button. This double inden-tation makes the left margin rather broad.

Example
We shall reduce this rather wide margin. The para-graph is probably still selected. If not, select it now. Click on the Decrease Indent button. The indentation is immediately reduced. Save the text under the same name FEATHER2.

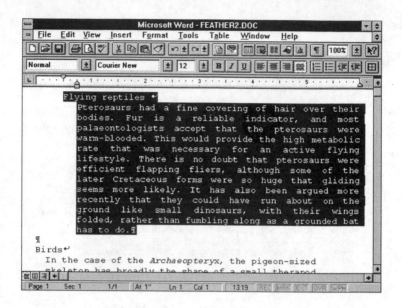

Assigning listing within paragraphs

The various paragraphs within a text can be assigned listing symbols to emphasize the contents or points.

Example
Our original FEATHERS text is ideal to illustrate how to apply bulleting. We shall therefore load the FEATHERS document and assign listing symbols to the paragraphs.

Now select the entire text. Then click on the Bullets button on the Formatting toolbar.

A so-called *bullet* is placed in front of each paragraph heading and left indentation is applied. The subsequent lines are automatically indented.

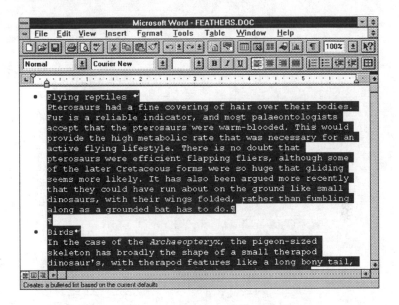

Save the text under the name FEATHBUL.

If you assign listing by means of the Bullets button, a dark square or spot is placed a quarter of an inch in front of the paragraphs. But you can apply a different symbol and a different distance if you like. This is done by selecting the *Bullets and Numbering* option from the *Format* menu.

Example
Instead of the standard symbol, we shall apply a hand with a pointing forefinger. This is to be found in the *Wingdings* character set. We shall also give it a point size of 14. This is done as follows:

■ Select the relevant paragraphs.
■ Open the *Format* menu.
■ Choose the *Bullets and Numbering* option.
■ If necessary, select the Bulleted tab sheet.

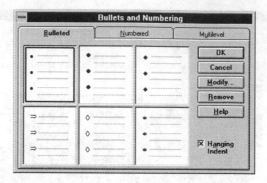

- Click on the Modify button.
- Change the value in the Point Size text box to 14.

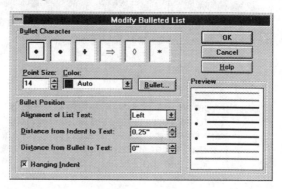

- Click on the Bullet button.
- Select Wingdings from the Symbols From options list.
- Select the eleventh symbol on the second row, the hand with the forefinger pointing right. The symbol is displayed larger when you click on it.

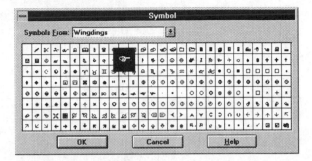

■ Click on the OK button. The selected symbol is shown in the first box in the Modify Bulleted List dialog box. The Preview box displays how the text will look with this symbol as the listing symbol.

The *Symbol* and *Wingdings* character sets provide many possibilities for applying special features to the text. These character sets can also be opened using the *Font* option from the *Format* menu.

Save the text under the name FEATHFIN.

You can remove the bullets and the corresponding indentation by activating the Remove button in the Bullets and Numbering dialog box.

Example
We shall remove the listing symbols once more. This is done as follows:

■ Select all the paragraphs with listing symbols.
■ Open the Bullets and Numbering dialog window by selecting this option from the *Format* menu.
■ Click on the Remove button.

Numbering the paragraphs

You can also automatically number paragraphs by means of the Formatting toolbar.

Example
We shall number the paragraphs in our FEATHFIN
document. This is done as follows:

- Select the relevant paragraphs.
- Click on the Numbering button on the Formatting
  toolbar.

The numbering automatically replaces the bullet symbols. When this method is applied, the paragraphs are
given a standard left-alignment, which means that in
cases of numbers with two figures, the text is indented
but the numbers themselves are not placed exactly under one another.

```
Courier 10 pts
8.  Text
    Text
9   Text
    Text
10.    Text
    Text
11.    Text
    Text
```

```
Courier 12 pts
8.  Text
    Text
9.  Text
    Text
10.    Text
    Text
11.    Text
    Text
```

Times New Roman 10 pts
8. Text
    Text
9. Text
    Text
10. Text
    Text
11. Text
    Text

Times New Roman 12 pts
8. Text
    Text
9. Text
    Text
10. Text
    Text
11. Text
    Text

When applying automatic numbering, you have to keep in mind that indentation occurs by a distance of 0.25 inches. This corresponds to 3 characters with a point size of 10 and 2.5 characters with a point size of 12, so there may be irregularity in the listing due to the spacing required.

Save the text under the name FEATHNUM.

If you wish to apply non-standard numbering or hyphenated numbering, or if the numbering has to begin with a number other than 1, select the *Bullets and Numbering* option from the *Format* menu. Click on the Modify button in the Numbered tab sheet. In the subsequent Modify Numbered List dialog window, it is also possible to alter any negative indentation.

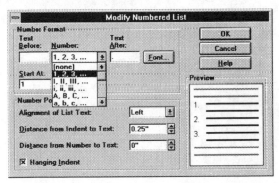

The Number options list provides various options:

Types of numbering:

1	2	3 ...
I	II	III ...
i	ii	iii ...
A	B	C ...
a	b	c ...
1st	2nd ...	
One	Two ...	
First	Second ...	

You can specify one or more special characters in front of and behind the layout character, and the character itself can be assigned a different font, font attribute and font size than the normal text.

Attention: Each formatting feature which is applied to a paragraph is assigned to the paragraph marking. If you remove this character, you remove all formatting from the relevant paragraph.

The Format Painter button enables you to copy paragraph formatting to other paragraphs. To do this, select the paragraph mark of the relevant paragraph. Subsequently, you only need to place the Painter in the required paragraph in order to copy the format.

Checking the paragraph and character formatting

You can check the paragraph and character formatting quite simply by means of the Help button on the Standard toolbar. Place the mouse pointer with the question mark on the position you wish to check and press the left mouse button. Information about the paragraph and character formatting in the selected area will then be displayed in a window. Switch the Help function off by clicking on the question mark once more.

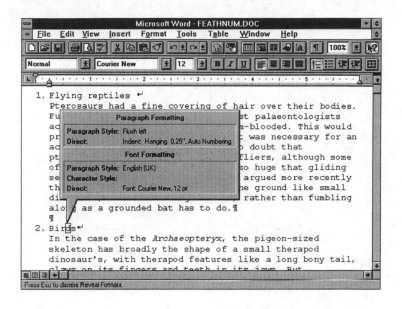

Exercise 6c

1   Enter the shortcut keys used for the following paragraph formatting functions:

Reducing the left indent by one tab stop _____

Justifying _____

Centring _____

Line spacing at one and a half _____

2   Place a cross next to the correct statements about the Ruler shown below:

The Ruler is activated in the Options dialog window. ☐

The Ruler layout is always set to 10 characters per inch. ☐

You can only use the Ruler for formatting if you have a mouse. ☐

You can specify both left and right indentation using the Ruler. Negative indentation is
also possible.   □

3   In the report of the meeting of the Board of Direc-
     tors, the following points on the agenda were re-
     corded:

     1.   The Chairman gave a summary of the events of
          the previous financial year, including an
          indication of the current company prospects
          ...
     2.   ...

     Which actions should be carried out here?

     _____
     _____
     _____

     Which problems arise if there are more than nine
     points on the agenda?

     _____
     _____

4   In your PRINTER document, apply the corre-
     sponding appearance to the fonts mentioned, in
     other words, allocate 'Arial 8 pts' its own font, and
     the others their own fonts. Save the result as
     PRINT3.DOC.

Answers 6c

1   Enter the shortcut keys used for the following par-
    agraph formatting functions:

Reducing the left indent by one tab stop	*Ctrl-Shift-M*
Justifying	*Ctrl-J*
Centring	*Ctrl-E*
Line spacing at one and a half	*Ctrl-5*

2   Place a cross next to the correct statements about
    the Ruler shown below:

The Ruler is activated in the Options dialog
window.   ☐
The Ruler layout is always set to 10 charac-
ters per inch.   ☐
You can only use the Ruler for formatting if
you have a mouse.   ☒
You can specify both left and right indenta-
tion using the Ruler. Negative indentation is
also possible.   ☒

3   In the report of the meeting of the Board of Direc-
    tors, the following points on the agenda were re-
    corded:

1. The Chairman gave a summary of the events of
    the previous financial year, including an
    indication of the current company prospects
    ...

2. ...

Which actions should be carried out here?

*Select the paragraphs and click on the Numbering
button on the Formatting toolbar.*

Which problems arise if there are more than nine points on the agenda?

Numbering as always left-aligned. Thus, when double figures are reached, the numbers are no longer exactly underneath one another.
If the point size is 12 points or more, the first line of the paragraph will be indented too far to the right.

4   Allocate the appropriate fonts. The result should be as follows:

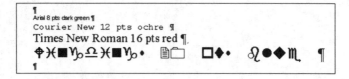

6.5   Placing text in columns

You probably never think about it, but you encounter text in columns every day in newspapers and magazines. This feature can be very convenient for your own documents; you may wish, for example, to place two alternatives side by side.

We shall discuss the column feature using a letter which recently appeared in the Washington Post.

```
Dear Sir,

Violence is a distasteful and often extremely dis-
tressing matter. It is with an, albeit miniature,
sigh of relief that we now witness the long overdue
United Nations military intervention in former Yugo-
slavia. In the face of an excess of totally unac-
ceptable civilian deaths and torture, we must surely
ask ourselves how the heartless turds in Foreign Of-
fices throughout the world have been able to prolong
their political careers by selling hot air on such a
```

scale to the media for so long. Kuwait appeared to
be subject to other rules.

Now that the weapons ultimatum has proved to be successful in curbing the danger to innocent civilians,
I suggest that the United Nations should now con-
sider intervention in Washington and Los Angeles.
Armed citizens could be given 10 days to surrender
their weapons to the authorities, otherwise armed
troops could be instructed to take swift and severe
combative action. The cities could be surrounded to
enforce a weapons embargo.

Or are we going to accept needless civilian suffer-
ing and death because politicians are still busy
with their own futures?

Yours faithfully, Frederick Douglass.

Creating columns by means of menu commands

Example
Type the text as shown. Place the introduction and
closing passage in boldface. Save the text under the
name INTERVNT.

The text is to be reproduced in two columns side by
side, both on the screen and on the printer. A vertical
line is to be placed between the columns.

This is done as follows:

- Select the text excepting the introduction and the
  closing passage.
- Open the *Format* menu.
- Select the *Columns* option.
- Select Two in the Presets section. Or you can increase the number in the Number of Columns text
  box.
- Ensure that a cross in displayed in the Equal Column Width check box.

- Selected Text should be shown in the Apply To box.
- Ensure a cross is displayed in the Line Between check box.

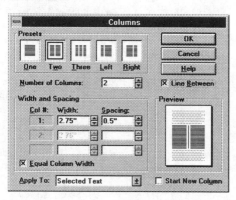

You can alter the standard width between the columns in intervals of 0.1". If you do not activate the Equal Column Width option, you can specify the column width yourself. When you have altered the width of the first column, the width of the second column is automatically calculated. This dialog window also provides standard settings for texts in two columns with different widths.

- Click on OK.

The text is shown in one column! In normal display, a double broken line will appear in the document window in front of and behind the selected text to indicate the *section breaks*. This indicates the section of the text which will be split into columns.

If you now activate the page display by means of the *Page Layout* option from the *View* menu, the text will appear in columns on the screen. You can also switch to page display by clicking on the Page Layout View button (lower left on the horizontal scroll bar, second from the left). You can switch back to the normal display by clicking on the first button on this scroll bar.

The columns are arranged so that they are equal in length wherever possible; the selected text is divided correspondingly.

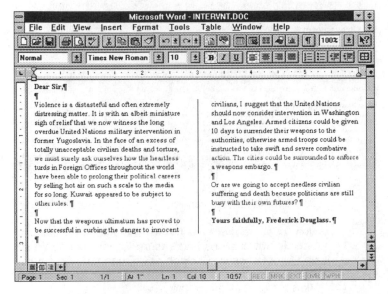

This was a straightforward example, but it may occur that when you split text into columns, you might wish to have a different point of division.

Example

We shall load the PRINT2 text and divide it into columns. Do this as follows:

Load the document and allocate a 12 point bold font to the title. Give an 11 point bold font to the headings, 'Impact Printers' and 'Non-Impact printers' and underline them. Place the other subheadings in boldface.

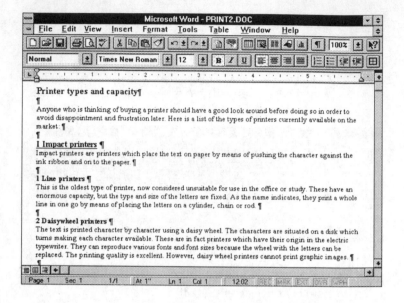

Select the text, beginning at 'I Impact printers'.

Now open the *Format* menu and choose *Columns*.
Specify two columns and ensure Equal Column Width
and Line Between. Click on OK. Open the *View* menu
and select *Page Layout* or click on the Page Layout
View button to examine the result.

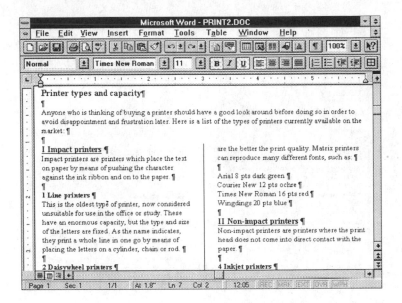

In this case, we wish to have the Impact printers in one column and the Non-Impact printers in the other. This is done as follows:

- Place the insertion point just in front of where the second column is to begin (II Non-Impact printers).
- Open the *Insert* menu.
- Select the *Break* option.

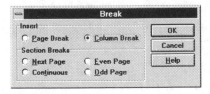

- Activate the *Column Break* option button.
- Click on OK.

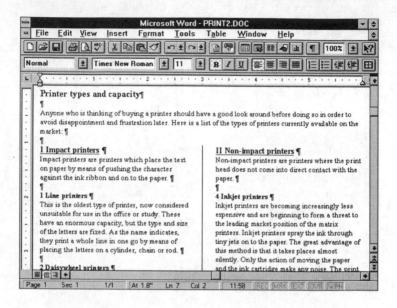

An easy way of making the column split at the required position is to place the insertion point just in front of the desired second column and then press Ctrl-Shift-Enter.

Save the document as PRINTCOL.

Specifying columns using the Standard toolbar

The Standard toolbar provides the Columns button, enabling you to display text in columns quickly and easily.

Example
Load the FEATHFIN text.

In order to display the text in two columns, proceed as follows:

- Select the text.
- Click on the Columns button in the Standard tool-bar. A larger button with four columns appears on the screen.
- Place the mouse pointer on the first column.
- Drag the mouse pointer to the second column.
- Release the mouse button.

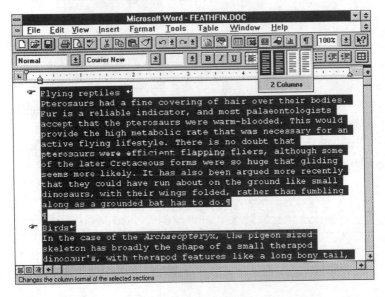

In this case too, the selected text is only displayed in columns on the screen when the Page Layout View is activated.

6.6   Hyphenation

The appearance of the text can often be improved by applying temporary hyphenation in lengthy words. When a word does not fit on to a line, it will have to be hyphenated or moved to the next line as a whole. Particularly when working with columns, you will notice that hyphenation should be applied to keep the right edge of the text straight instead of ragged.

Automatic hyphenation

A good word processor should provide a function for automatic hyphenation.

Example
We shall illustrate how this works by formatting the FEATHERS text.

We wish to display this text in three columns as in a newspaper or magazine, just for practice. To make it more newspaper-like, we shall allocate boldface to the headings

- Select the headings and click on the Bold button on the Formatting toolbar.
- Select the entire text by pressing F8 five times.
- Click on the Columns button on the Standard toolbar.
- Click on the left column and drag the mouse pointer to the third column before releasing it.
- Activate the Page Layout View.
- Apply full justification by clicking on the Justify button on the Formatting toolbar (the most right of the alignment buttons).

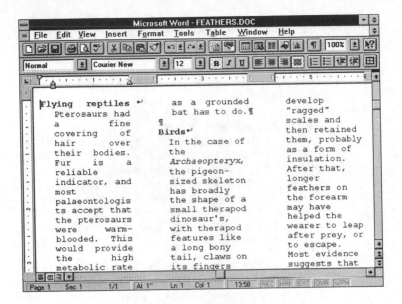

As you see, the text layout is rather ragged with large spaces between words here and there. The division of words is also rather bizarre.

We shall apply automatic hyphenation of the text.

- Press Ctrl-Home to move to the beginning of the text.
- Open the *Tools* menu.
- Select the *Hyphenation* option.

The Hyphenation dialog window appears over the text.

- Activate the Automatically Hyphenate Document option.

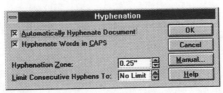

The Hyphenate Words in CAPS option enables you to specify whether or not words consisting exclusively of capitals should be hyphenated.
If you activate the Automatically Hyphenate Document option, the hyphenation will indeed take place fully automatically.

The default setting for the Hyphenation Zone is 0.25". This hyphenation zone refers to the distance from the right-hand margin within which Word will attempt to place a word, where it would otherwise remain empty. If you are working with the Times New Roman font (the default Word setting), this distance corresponds to four or five characters. If you are using a larger font than the default 10 point size, you should increase the size of the hyphenation zone.

Although Word is very thorough in its knowledge of hyphenation, not all possibilities can be included in its files. Words can often be hyphenated at several places; you should check these yourself and apply manual hyphenation if the need arises. In addition, automatic hyphenation may be applied which results in untidy or undesired text layout. If you wish to apply manual hyphenation, click on the Manual button in the Hyphenation dialog window.

The text is automatically shown in the Page Layout mode (*View* menu). In the Manual Hyphenation text box, the word to be hyphenated is shown along with the possible hyphenation. The suggested position is accentuated. You can accept this by selecting Yes or you can alter it using the mouse or the cursor keys. When the Hyphenation dialog window has been closed, the screen is displayed in the original mode once more.

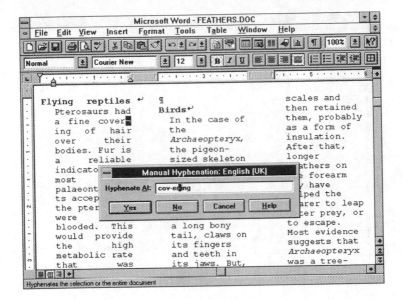

Example

We shall now hyphenate the FEATHERS text. The text should appear as shown in the figure below.

- Select *Hyphenation* from the *Tools* menu.
- Activate the Automatically Hyphenate Document option button.
- Click on OK.

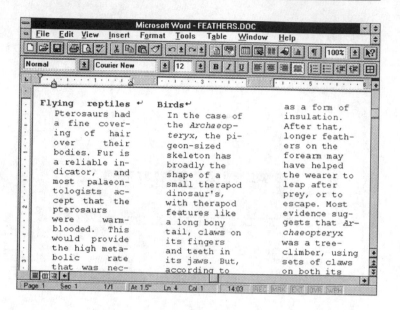

In reverse, it may occur that you wish to have certain
terms or expressions given as entities and therefore
not hyphenated. For instance, a measurement of '72 x
36 in.' should be regarded as a whole. Word is not allowed to split it, even at one of the three spaces con-
tained. When typing this measurement, you should use
fixed spaces. These are placed by pressing Ctrl-Shift-
Spacebar instead of just the spacebar.

When the hyphen is used as a linking sign, for instance
in the statement 'Children 5-16 years', the intention is
to keep the numbers together. This can be done by applying a fixed hyphen. In that case, press Ctrl-Shift-hy-
phen.

Exercise 6d

1 You wish to apply automatic hyphenation in a text and confirm each suggestion. Which commands have to be given?

_____

_____

_____

_____

2 Load the FEATHERS text and add the text shown below. Give the entire text a 10 points font size, divide it into three columns and hyphenate it automatically. Save it under the name FEATH3.

It was once debated whether such a reptile-like bird as *Archaeopteryx* could have managed to fly. For example, it does not have a deep breastbone, which, in modern birds, is the site of attachment of the powerful flight muscles. Without a breastbone, surely it lacked the muscle to beat its wings? The whole question now seems rather ludicrous; after all, why should *Archaeopteryx* have had feathers and wings if it could not have flown? Indeed the feathers are those of a flyer. Further, modern bats do not have a deep breastbone, and yet they fly perfectly well. The other debate, which is not resolved, concerns whether birds evolved flight from the trees down (i.e. by leaping from branch to branch, and flapping as a means to leap yet further) or from the ground up (i.e. by running and hopping after insect prey and flapping to achieve greater leaps).

Answers 6d

1   You wish to apply automatic hyphenation in a text
    and confirm each suggestion. Which commands
    have to be given?

    Press Ctrl-Home.
    Open the Tools menu.
    Select the Hyphenation option.
    Press Enter or click on OK.

2   Load the FEATHERS text and add the text shown
    below. Give the entire text a 10 points font size, di-
    vide it into three columns and hyphenate it auto-
    matically. Save it under the name FEATH3.

    *As you will have seen, you can type the new text
    under the existing text. It is automatically placed in
    a column. When you have done this, select the en-
    tire text by pressing F8 five times. Click on the 10
    points font size in the Formatting toolbar. Open the
    Tools menu and select Hyphenation. Ensure that
    the Automatic Hyphenation is activated. Click on
    OK. Subsequently, click on the Justify button on
    the Formatting toolbar. Click on the Columns but-
    ton on the Standard toolbar. Activate the Page
    Layout View (View menu) to see the result:*

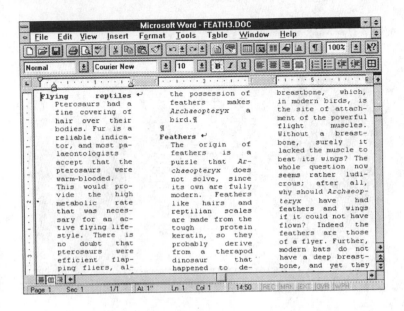

6.7 Print Preview

The document window can only show a part of a real page. You can only gain a view of the entire page if you activate the *Print Preview* option from the *File* menu.

- Open the *File* menu.
- Select the *Print Preview* option.

You can also activate the Print Preview window by clicking on the Print Preview button on the Standard toolbar. That is the fifth button from the left.

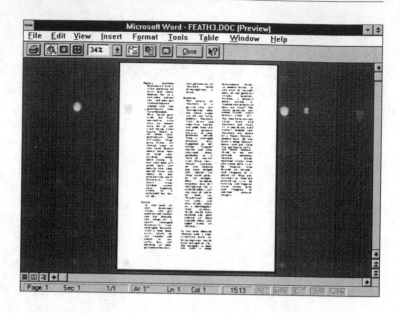

The toolbar in the Print Preview window provides the
following buttons and boxes, from left to right:

  Print   Activating this button will print the text ac-
                                      cording to the currently valid settings. In
                                      that case, it is not possible to alter the set-
                                      tings.

  Magnifier   It is not possible initially to edit text in the
                                      Print Preview window. However, the Mag-
                                      nifier works as a kind of switch between
                                      zooming in and out and editing. If the but-
                                      ton has been activated, click with the loop
                                      mouse pointer on the required text position
                                      to examine it more closely. If you then click
                                      on the Magnifier, the insertion point ap-
                                      pears in the text enabling you to carry out
                                      modifications. This is convenient for ad-
                                      justing the page layout and for positioning
                                      frames and figures.

  One Page   Clicking on this button places one page on
                                      the screen.

Multiple Pages — Clicking on this button enables you to display between one and seven pages simultaneously on the screen.

 Zoom Control — This facility enables you to display the document is various sizes on the screen.

 View Ruler — This button activates the horizontal and vertical Ruler in the Print Preview window.

 Shrink To Fit — This button reduces the font size so that the document is shortened by one page.

 Full Screen — This button increases the screen display area by removing the menu bar, the toolbar and the status bar from the screen.

Close button — This button switches you back to the Word document window.

 Help — This button activates help text. The mouse pointer assumes the shape of this button. Place the mouse pointer at the position on the screen about which you wish to gain more information and click on the left mouse button. If you click in the document, a window will appear providing information about the formatting of characters and paragraphs.

Exercise 6e

1   Type the following text and format it as shown. Couple the subheadings to their paragraphs by pressing Shift-Enter instead of Enter to create a new line. Save it under the name MUTATE.

<u>Flesh</u>
Despite the seriousness of the actual problems, vegetarians may have secretly been feeling a little smug as reports about 'mad cow disease' and bovine aids appeared in the media. This has given fuel to their arguments that vegetarianism is a much more healthy way of life. But recent reports from the agrarian sector are beginning to indicate that not all is well in the realm of plants.

Mutation

Plants appear to be subject to spontaneous mutation
and scientists are still puzzled about the reasons
why. Two particular cases which closely concern hu-
man consumption are the newly discovered cases of
'wheat fatigue' and the so-called 'raving lettuce
leaf syndrome'.

Fatigue

Wheat fatigue seems to arrive almost overnight, af-
fecting wheat which is ready to be harvested. The
heads of grain begin to hang down and if left long
enough, the stem will droop and eventually break. It
has been discovered that consumption of bread and
pasta products such as spaghetti and lasagne made
from this wheat, will cause feelings of tiredness
and listlessness in the consumer - "like a stone in
my stomach" as one victim complained. A few days in
bed is inevitably the result. It has also been discovered that the only known antidote to this is
rapid consumption of voluminous quantities of young
red wine. It is debatable whether the illness or the
cure is the more serious.

RALLS

A potentially more hazardous threat to the popula-
tion is comes from the 'raving lettuce leaf
syndrome' (RALLS). For no apparent reason, some
plants produce leaves which deviate strongly from
the normal structure, often assuming shapes of objects in the nearby surroundings. Consumption of
these leaves produces a powerful but temporary hal-
lucinatory effect, comparable to LSD or XTC. The
Ministry of Health is considering a ban on these
plants while research goes on into the causes of the
mutation. Theories at the moment indicate that
ground pollution and excessive noise (pop music in
particular) may be factors which accelerate this
process.

(From *Health and Wealth*, Sept. 1994)

2   The last two paragraphs in the text are to be placed in columns, side by side. The space between the columns is to be one inch. Which commands are required to implement this?

---

3   Eliminate the ragged right edge as much as possible by activating the automatic hyphenation function. Then save the text as MUTATE2.

4   Jot down the commands which are needed to place a two-page print preview on the screen.

Answers 6e

1   *The text when typed should initially look like this:*

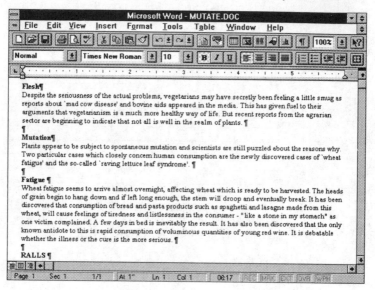

2   The last two paragraphs in the text are to be placed in columns, side by side. The space between the columns is to be one inch. Which commands are required to implement this?

Select the appropriate two paragraphs. Open the Format menu and choose the Columns option. The Presets section should be set to Two. Specify the spacing as 1". Ensure that Selected Text is chosen in the Apply To section. Click on the Line Between check box. Click on OK.

Place the mouse pointer just in front of the heading 'RALLS' and select Break from the Insert menu. Then select Column Break and click on OK.

3   Eliminate the ragged right edge as much as possi-

ble by activating the automatic hyphenation function. Then save the text as MUTATE2.

*Select the entire text and click on the Justify button
in the Formatting toolbar. While the text is still selected, open the Tools menu and select Hyphenation. Click on the Automatically Hyphenate Document option. The result should correspond to the
figure below.*

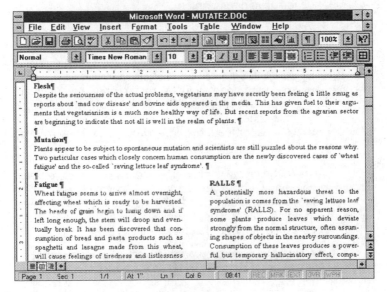

4   Jot down the commands which are needed to
place a two-page print preview on the screen.

Open the File menu.
Select the Print Preview option.
*Click on the fourth button from the left (Multiple
Pages) and drag the mouse pointer from the top
left-hand page to the second page. 1 x 2 pages will
be shown.*

6.8   Formatting pages

In addition to functions for character and paragraph formatting, Word also provides functions for Page formatting. Word is normally geared to a standard paper setting of 11 inches by 8.25 inches. However, this will
produce problems if you are working with pin-feed
paper which is twelve inches in length. The text will no
longer correspond to the page boundaries after several
pages have been printed.

The Word Page Setup function enables you to alter the
paper size, along with a number of other settings:

- the left, right, top and bottom margins
- the print orientation: Word can print the document
  in portrait or landscape orientation (down or across
  the page)
- the paper feed: to print envelopes for instance, you
  need to adjust the settings.

The page layout is altered by means of the *Page Setup*
command from the *File* menu. Activating this option
produces a dialog window containing the tab sheets,
Margins, Paper Size, Paper Source and Layout. These
contain a number of default settings.

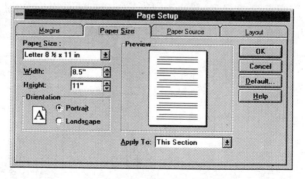

Example

We shall experiment with the PRINTER text to illustrate the page setup features.

Load the PRINTER text, select the entire text and give it a 12 points font size. This ensures that the text now occupies more than one page. Apply boldface to the headings to make them clearer. The easiest way of doing this is to select the first heading, click on the Bold button in the Formatting toolbar and then double click on the Format Painter in the Standard toolbar. As you select the other headings, they will be given this format. Click on the Format Painter once again to deactivate it.

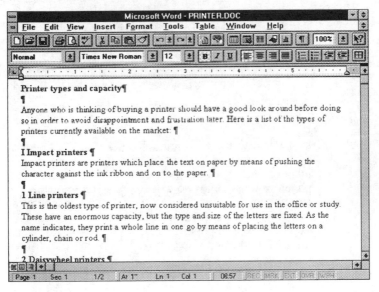

We shall change the top and bottom margins to 1.5". The page length will become 12". This is done as follows:

- Open the *File* menu.
- Select the *Page Setup* option.
- Select the Margins tab sheet if necessary.
- Change the value in the Top text box to 1.5". Type this value or click on the small triangle pointing upwards.
- Change the value in the Bottom text box to 1.5".
- Select the Paper Size tab sheet.
- Change the value in the Height box to 12".
- Click on OK or press Enter.

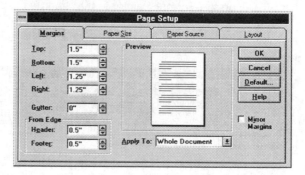

In addition to the four standard margins, the Margins tab sheet provides facilities for adding a binding margin and for distinguishing between left- and right-hand pages when printing two sides. A binding margin is an extra margin on one side of the paper for binding documents. The size is specified in the Gutter text box.

To print left- and right-hand pages differently, activate the Mirror Margins check box. When this option has been activated, the Left and Right options are converted to Inside and Outside.

If you are working with a printer in which various sizes of paper can be used, these will be shown in the Paper Size options list. This is the case, for instance, with different laser printers. The values in the Width and Height are adjusted to the selected option from the list. You can also manually adjust the values in these boxes if you wish.

Texts are normally printed in the Portrait orientation. But if you select the other option, Landscape, the values of the Width and Height are automatically adjusted. The Apply To options list enables you to apply the settings to the entire document, or to the section of the document from the current insertion point onwards. If you select a section of text in advance, it is possible to apply the settings to this section only.

The Default button will store the specified settings in the NORMAL.DOT file once you have confirmed the safeguard question. This file is used to assign the default settings to each new document. For instance, if you are working with a printer using 12" paper, it is advisable to specify this as the default setting.

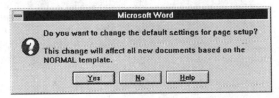

The precise appearance of the Paper Source tab sheet depends on the connected printer. If the printer possesses various input trays, you can determine whether or not different trays should be used for the first and subsequent pages.

Pagination

The General tab sheet in the Options dialog window (*Tools* menu) contains the Background Repagination check box. When you activate this option, Word automatically keeps track of the pagination. If you deactivate this option, pagination will take place when you switch back and forth between normal display and Page Layout View. This pagination appears in the normal display as a broken line.

Pagination occurs according to the specified paper size and margin settings. This may lead to undesired breaks in the text. In that case, page breaks can be applied manually by means of the key combination Ctrl-Enter at the position where the page break should occur. You can also specify the page breaks in the Break dialog window (*Insert* menu).

When the automatic Background Repagination option has been activated, you can format the paragraphs in such a way that no page breaks will be placed within them. The Text Flow tab sheet in the Paragraph dialog box (*Format* menu) provides the following options for this:

Widow/Orphan Control	This option prevents the last line of a paragraph being placed on the next page, or the first line of a paragraph being placed on a previous page. This setting is normally active.
Keep Lines Together	No pagination will occur in the middle of a paragraph.
Keep With Next	Two or more paragraphs belonging together will be printed on the same page.
Page Break Before	If a paragraph has been formatted using this option, a page break will be placed in front of the paragraph.

Example

We shall insert a page break in front of the second part of the PRINTER text, before Non-Impact printers. This is done as follows:

- Place the insertion point just in front of the heading 'Non-Impact printers'.
- Open the *Insert* menu and select *Break*.
- Activate the Page Break option.

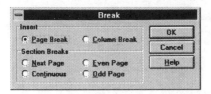

Save the document under the name PRINTBRK.

Adding bookmarks

In order to move quickly and easily to certain required positions in a lengthy text, it is convenient to place bookmarks at these positions. These are marks which are linked to key words. You could always find the word by means of the Search function, but this has the disadvantage that this function will find all the occurrences of the word throughout the text, not just the specific occurrence which we are looking for.

Example
Just for practice, we shall add bookmarks to the words 'lasagne' and 'music' in the MUTATE document. This is done as follows:

■ Select the word 'lasagne'.
■ Open the *Edit* menu.
■ Select the *Bookmark* option. The Bookmark dialog window appears. The cursor is blinking in the Bookmark Name text box.
■ Type the text 'lasagne' in the Bookmark Name box. Spaces and hyphens are not allowed in this name.
■ Press Enter or click on Add.

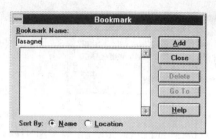

A bookmark has now been created for the first word. If you delete the word, the bookmark is also deleted. If you wish to delete only the bookmark, open the *Edit* menu once more, select the *Bookmark* option and highlight the name of the bookmark in the list under the text box. Then click on the Delete button.

Apply the same procedure to add the second word 'music'. Save the document under the name MUTE-MARK.DOC.

The Go To function

The bookmarks which you have just allocated are used, as mentioned, to find a certain position in the text. This is done by means of the Go To function. The procedure is as follows:

- Open the *Edit* menu.
- Select the *Go To* option. The Go To dialog window appears. You can select a page, line, bookmark etc. from the Go to What options list.
- Select the Bookmark option.
- Select the name 'music' from the Enter Bookmark Name list.
- Press Enter or click on the Go To button.
- Click on Close.

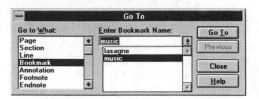

Printing sections of text

Pagination makes it possible to print sections of text instead of the entire document. Even if you do not display any page numbering on the screen, Word will keep track of this. You can make use of this via the Print dialog box (*File* menu).

Print What
This box normally shows Document, since in most cases the whole document is to be printed. However, you can specify that passages of text, remarks, summary info or other matters pertaining to the text are to be printed.

Copies
Specify the number of copies of the text which are to be printed.

Page Range

Specify the section of the text which is to be printed. Normally the All (thus the whole text) option is activated, but you can choose Current Page (the page where the insertion point is currently situated) or specify the required page numbers. For instance, if you wish to print pages 1, 3 and 5 to 7 type '1,3,5-7'. The Selection option is only active if you have already selected a section of text.

The Options button will open the Print tab sheet from the Options dialog box.

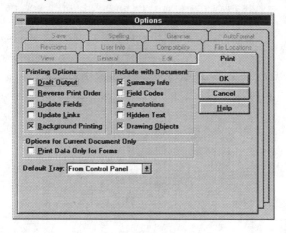

The options in this tab sheet have the following functions:

The Printing Options section

Draft Output
Documents are printed without special layout. Figures which have been adopted into the text are replaced by empty frames.

Reverse Print Order
The text is printed in reverse order of sequence, the last page being printed first. This is particularly convenient when the printer stacks the pages with the last printed page at the top.

Update Fields
Fields, such as the field for the current date for instance, are first modified before the printing process is set in motion. This option will be discussed in more detail in the section concerning fields.

Update Links
If a text contains components from another object (text, tables, figures), the corresponding data are first modified.

Background Printing
While the text is being dealt with by the printer, you can continue working with Word. However, a good section of working memory is used for this process and this will slow the computer down somewhat. It is advisable only to activate this option where necessary.

Include with Document section

Summary Info
Supplementary information relevant to the document will be printed if this option is active.

Field Codes
If this option is active, the codes for the fields themselves (such as DATE for instance) are printed instead of the results of the codes (such as 14-09-94).

Annotations
Any remarks concerning the document are printed when this option is active.

Hidden Text
Hidden text in the document will be printed.

Drawing Objects
You can adopt a simple drawing into Word. You can
determine if this drawing is to be printed along with the
rest of the text. The drawing remains visible on the
screen.

It is advisable not to activate these options as yet. Activate the Print Data Only for Forms option if you are
working with forms. This option enables you to specify
that only the data entered in the form are printed instead and not the form itself.

Example
We shall print the whole MUTATE text. This is done as
follows:

- Load the document if necessary.
- Select *Print* from the *File* menu.
- Select Document in the Print What section.
- Ensure that the All options button is activated in
  the Page Range section.
- Click on OK.

Exercise 6f

1   Load the PRINTBRK text from your work diskette.
    We shall give it a new format so remove the page
    break by moving the insertion point to it and press-
    ing the Del Key.

2   Format the text in line with the specifications be-
    low:

    top margin   2.5"
    bottom margin   1.5"
    left margin   2.5"
    right margin   2"
    paper   8$1/2$ x 11" automatic feed

3   Apply pagination in such a way that no paragraphs
    are internally split.

4   Create the following bookmarks:
    Paragraph 3 ('1 Line printers)   Oldest
    Paragraph 4 ('graphic images')   NoGraphic
    Paragraph 5 ('Matrix printers')   Popular
    Paragraph 7 ('quality')   Quality

5   Which commands are necessary to move the in-
    sertion point to the Popular bookmark?

    _____
    _____
    _____

6   Save the altered text under the name PRINTMAR.

Answers 6f

1,2

Load the document and delete the page break as explained. Open the File menu and select Page Setup. Specify the margins as required in the Margins tab sheet. Move to the Paper Size tab sheet and select Letter 8¹/2 x 11 in from the Paper Size drop-down list. Move to the Paper Source tab sheet and ensure that Auto Sheet is activated. Click on OK.

3   Apply pagination in such a way that no paragraphs are internally split.

Select the entire text by pressing F8 five times. Open the Format menu and choose Paragraph. Activate the Keep Lines Together option. Click on OK. Unfortunately, the page break lands between the heading Matrix printers and the relevant paragraph. Move the insertion point to just in front of the heading. Open the Insert menu, choose Break and activate the Page Break option. Click on OK. The page break is now moved.

4   Create the following bookmarks:

Select the word in the text. Open the Edit menu and select Bookmark. Type the name to be assigned. Click on the Add button.

Open the *File* menu and click on *Print Preview*. If you have given all the instructions as you should have, your text will now resemble the figure below.

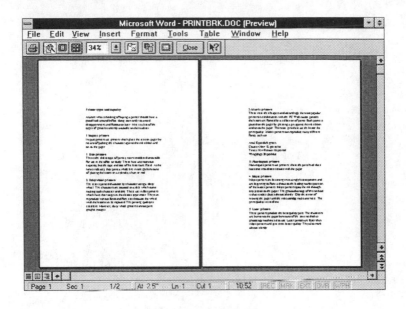

5　Which commands are necessary to move the insertion point to the Popular bookmark?

Open the Edit menu.
Select the Go To option.
Select the Bookmark option from the Go To list.
Open the Enter Bookmark Name drop-down list.
Select Popular from the list.
Click on Go To or press Enter.
Click on Close.

7   Good impressions
Writing the right letter

An advanced word processor provides facilities for pro-
ducing the right document at the right time. Letters,
both business and private, are nowadays often created
using a word processing program. Their appearance
can be of some importance. They function as a kind of
visiting card and therefore should be attractive and
easy to read. We shall use the text structure shown below to illustrate some of the features we shall discuss in
this chapter.

```
Gnasher Clark
69 Charnel Ave
Dover DV3 4HP
¶
¶
¶
¶
¶
{ Title } { Name }
{ Number } { Street }
{ Town } { Postal Code }
{ Country }
¶
¶
¶
{ Subject: }
{ Reference: }
¶
      Dover, { PRINTDATE \@ 'd mmmm yyyy' \* MERGEFORMAT }
{ }
¶
Yours sincerely,
¶
¶
¶
¶
Supplements:
{ }
¶
```

We shall construct this letter from Mr. Clark step by step. You can subsequently adapt the empty letter template to your own requirements and save it for future use.

Normally the A4 paper size (11" x 8.25") is used for letters, but you may have 12" pin-feed paper in your printer. If so, you will have to adjust the settings. This is done as follows:

- Open the *File* menu.
- Select *Page Setup*.
- Activate the Paper Size tab sheet and change the Height.
- Click on OK or press Enter.

A normal letter has a left margin of 10 characters (1"). The right margin should be equal to 5 characters (0.5"). The top and bottom margins are both equal to 1".

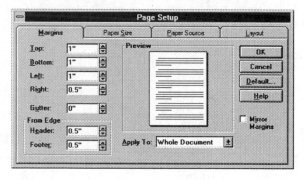

If you wish your own work to correspond to the examples in this book, use the Page Setup dialog window to specify these settings. Select the Times New Roman 10 pts font.

7.1   The letter heading

Companies make use of paper which already has a logo. In our example, we shall have to create something here ourselves or leave this area blank. In our example, we have typed the address of the sender on the first three lines. You can add a telephone number on the fourth line if you wish.

Five empty lines are left above the area in which the data of the recipient are to be placed. This position should be specified exactly, so that the letter can also be inserted into a window envelope.

7.2   The recipient

The window in a common window envelope is something like 1.5" by 4". This means that you can show a maximum of seven lines. In practice, it is handy not to use the first or last lines because letters sometimes shift a little in the envelope if they are folded compactly. Five lines are usually sufficient to type the name and address of the recipient.

To ensure that you will not forget any data, you can enter fields here which will serve as an aid to memory. It is advisable to define the fields contents simply and clearly; you can use them later when we discuss the creation of form letters. An additional advantage of these fields is that you can activate them using the F11 function key or the Alt-F1 key combination when you are actually writing the letter. Proceed as follows:

- Place the insertion point at line 9.
- Press Ctrl-F9. Two braces, enclosing the insertion point, appear on the screen.
- Type 'Title' between the braces.
- Select the text between the braces (only the text!) and press Ctrl-Shift-H. The text between the braces has to be hidden, otherwise an error message will appear.
- Place the insertion point behind the closing brace and type a space.

- Press Ctrl-F9 again.
- Type 'Name' between the brackets.
- Hide the text again as you did with 'Title'.

You have now created two fields where you can enter the title (Dr., Professor, or simply Mr. or Mrs.) and the actual name.

Now create fields for 'Number', 'Street', 'Town', 'Postal Code', and 'Country' in the same way on lines 10, 11 and 12.

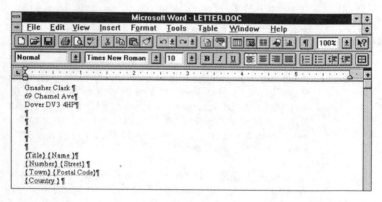

7.3   Subject and reference number

The number of blank lines you insert after the area with all the address data largely depends on the final text layout and thus on the volume of text in the letter. Between the data of the recipient (which will appear in the envelope window) and the rest of the letter there should be at least one blank line. In our example we shall place 'Subject:' on line 16. This is so that you can fill in key words concerning the letter contents. The 'Reference:' will be placed on line 17.

You can also enter these as fields so that they will not automatically appear in the printed letter.

7.4   Registration of place and date

Subsequently, the place and date should be specified. First create a blank line by pressing Enter. Both these registrations are often right-aligned in letters. You can again make use of a field here. When the letter is printed, the field code is replaced by the current date. A right-aligned date field is placed as follows:

- Place the insertion point at line 19.
- Type the location, followed by a comma and space.
- Open the *Insert* menu.
- Select the *Field* option. Then select *Date and Time* from the Categories list.
- Select the PrintDate option from the Field Names list.
- Click on the Options button and select the required date format such as dd MMMM yyyy for instance.
- Click on the Add to Field button.

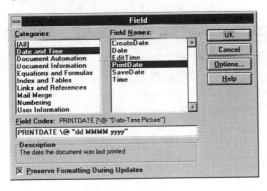

- Click on the OK button and, in the Field dialog box, on OK again.
- Click on the Right-Align button on the Formatting toolbar.

In the subsequent paragraph, you will have to restore the left-alignment for the text. That is done in a similar way.

The date indication '00 XXX 0000' is shown on the screen. Because Word does not know on which date the letter will be printed, it cannot enter any data here as yet. You can see that this represents a field by opening the *Tools* menu, selecting *Options* and activating the Field Codes option in the View tab sheet. The zeros and Xs are replaced by the code {PRINT-DATE\@"dd MMMM yyyy" *MERGEFORMAT}. Between the braces, the field type and the date format are registered. In this format the date will be printed as '08 September 1994'.

7.5   The intro

Skip two lines. You can also use an empty field for the introduction; this helps you remember that the introduction is to be placed at this position. In (business) letters the intro almost always begins with 'Dear' and is closed with a comma. Therefore both of these can be placed around the field.

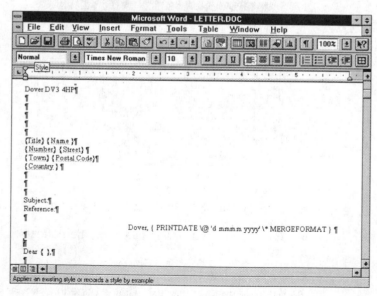

7.6   The actual text

Skip a line after the intro. If you wish, you can also place an empty field on the first line where the text is to be typed, although very few will forget to write the letter.

7.7   Conclusion and signature

The conclusion 'Yours faithfully' or 'Yours sincerely' will be separated from the text by a blank line. Leave three or four lines empty for your signature.

7.8   Supplements

It is advisable to specify not only the number of supplements you enclose along with the letter, but to name them as well. This can turn out to be important particularly in correspondence with large companies. The post is often opened by the secretary before being passed on to the appropriate department so that the chance of losing a page or two does exist.

We shall reserve the bottom two lines of the letter for noting the supplements. Therefore on the third line from the bottom we shall place the 'Supplements:' field.

Calculating backwards, this means that the conclusion will be placed on the seventh or eighth line from the bottom margin.

In reality of course, you will write letters to fit your own requirements. The number of blank lines will depend on the volume of text.

The texts between braces in the field codes should be given the Hidden format, otherwise they will be interpreted as codes for creating a form letter. In that case, an error message will be displayed.

Example

We shall now define the text between the braces as hidden. This is done as follows:

- Select a text (in a field) which is not yet hidden.
- Press Ctrl-Shift-H.
- Double click on the Format Painter button on the Standard toolbar.
- Select the other fields one by one. The hidden format is applied to each.

Save the letter in its current form under the name LET-STRUC.

In order to see on paper which fields you have used, you can print this letter in a special way:

- Open the *File* menu.
- Select the *Print* command.
- Click on the Options button.
- Activate the Field Codes check box in the Include with Document section.
- Also activate the Hidden Text check box in the same section.
- Click on OK. Click on OK once more to actually start the printing process.

Switch these options off again when you print your real letters, otherwise you will always get the field codes in your letters as well as the information you place there.

Entering the address data

When you type a letter using the template, press F11 or Alt-F1 when you have loaded the template in Word. The first field (Title) is then selected. Press the Cursor Right key to move the insertion point to behind the field. Because these field texts will not be printed, you can simply ignore them. Type the relevant addressee text. Subsequently press F11 again to move to the next field.

Note

It is very easy to make mistakes. It may happen that you press F11 or Alt-F1 and begin to type straightaway. This may result in the fields being overwritten. This is certainly not our intention. To make this impossible, open *Tools* menu, select *Options* and activate the Edit tab sheet. Ensure that there is no cross in the Typing Replaces Section box. Click on OK.

You can skip a field by pressing F11 twice. The field remains on the screen but it will not be printed. For instance, you need not always type Great Britain on all your letters. If you skip a field unintentionally, press Shift-F11 or Alt-Shift-F1 to go back to it.

Exercise 7a

Write a letter using the following data:

Sender
Gnasher Clark
69 Charnel Ave
Dover DV3 4HP

Recipient
Lector's Adult Toys Ltd.
14-15 Tiger Mews
Bognor BG2 5CD

Contents
Gnasher Clark has ordered an inflatable doll ('Dream 17') from Lector's mailing company. On delivery, the doll appears to be poorly finished. There is no evidence of damage in transit. Reclaim the costs from the mailing company.

Save the letter under the name DOLL.DOC.

Answer 7a

The structure of the exercise is shown below. It is important that you switch off the Field Codes display again before actually printing the letter.

```
┌─────────────────────────────────────────────────────────────────┐
│                    Microsoft Word - DOLL.DOC                 ▼ ♦ │
│ File  Edit  View  Insert  Format  Tools  Table  Window  Help  ♦ │
│ ▢▢▢ ▢▢▢ ✕▢▢▢ ▢±▢± ▢▢ ▢▢▢▢▢▢ ▢ 100% ± ▢? │
│ Normal    ± Times New Roman ± 10 ± B I U ▢▢▢▢ ▢▢▢▢ ▢ │
│ └X····1····1····2····1····3····1····4····1····5····1···· △ · ♦│
│                                                                   │
│   Gnasher Clark ¶ ▪                                               │
│   69 Chamel Ave¶                                                  │
│   Dover DV3 4HP¶                                                  │
│   ¶                                                               │
│   ¶                                                               │
│   ¶                                                               │
│   {Title}{Name } Lector's Adult Toys Ltd. ¶                       │
│   {Number} 14-15 {Street} Tiger Mews ¶                            │
│   {Town} Bognor {Postal Code} BG25CD¶                             │
│   {Country }¶                                                     │
│   ¶                                                               │
│   ¶                                                               │
│   ¶                                                               │
│   Subject: Faulty doll¶                                           │
│   Reference: Dream 17¶                                            │
│   ¶                                                               │
│                       Dover, {PRINTDATE \@ "dd MMMM yyyy" \* MERGEFORMAT }¶ │
│   ¶                                                               │
│   ¶                                                               │
│   Dear { }Mr Lector,¶                                             │
│ ▣▣▣◆                                                          ♦ │
│ Page 1   Sec 1    1/1    At 1"   Ln 1   Col 7    12:52  ▢▢▢▢▢▢ │
└─────────────────────────────────────────────────────────────────┘
```

The rest of the text is as follows:

Gnasher Clark
69 Charnel Ave
Dover DV3 4HP

Lector's Adult Toys Ltd.
14-15 Tiger Mews
Bognor BG2 5CD

Subject: Faulty doll
Reference: Dream 17

Dover, 08 September 1994

Dear Mr Lector,

I was delighted and excited yesterday when the delivery service rang and delivered the package that I ordered from your company a couple of weeks ago.

However, my delight quickly turned to frustration when I actually got to grips with the doll. Instead of a firm smooth substance, I was landed with a pulpy, wrinkled object - there was clearly a leak somewhere which precluded the tight gleaming surface for which I was longing. There was however no sign of damage in transit, the plastic packing was hermetically sealed. Eventually I thought I had traced the leak and patched it, which gave the doll a rather charming, vulnerable appearance as if a plaster had been applied. However, this proved to be insufficient, and I discovered further leakage along the seam at a spot where repair was impossible. This is clearly a matter of faulty manufacture. Of course, the delivery service was long gone, so I had no chance of questioning him about the transit.

Of course, I do not like to complain. I would be much more contented to have a quiet night at home with a glass of wine and dinner for two. Unfortunately, in my opinion, the doll is beyond repair and I feel that I am entitled to a new one. Please don't get me wrong, I'm not the kind of person who just flits from one to the other.

I hope that you can help me, and therefore thank you in advance.

Yours sincerely,

7.9   Writing professional letters

Using the many formatting features in Word, we are able to design an attractive letter heading. The figure below shows a letter template with the letter heading for Lector's Adult Toys Ltd.

Lector's Adult Toys Ltd
14-15 Tiger Mews
Bognor BG2 5CD
Telephone 0243-222-4321

```
{ Title } { Name }
{ Number } { Street }
{ Town } { Postal Code }
{ Country }



Your Ref:  Your Letter Dated:  Our Ref:  Our Letter Dated:
{ Your Ref }


                                        Bognor, 0 XXX 0000

Dear { },


.....



Yours Sincerely,



Supplements:
{ }
```

Type the letter heading on the first four lines of the letter:

```
Lector's Adult Toys Ltd.
14-15 Tiger Mews
Bognor BG2 5CD
Telephone 0243-222-4321
```

Select the four lines and apply boldface. Centre the lines by means of the Centre button on the Formatting toolbar. Now select the first line and format it in the Times New Roman 14 pts font. Then replace the word 'Telephone' with the telephone symbol. This is done as follows:

- Double click on the word 'Telephone' to select it.
- Open the *Insert* menu.
- Select the *Symbol* option.
- Select the Symbols tab sheet if necessary.
- Select the Wingdings option from the Font list.
- Click on the ninth symbol from the left on the first line. The telephone symbol is shown magnified on the screen.
- Click on the Insert button and then on Close.

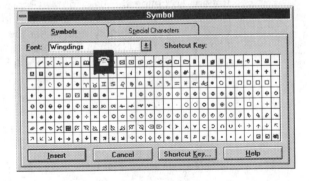

Now enter five blank lines down to the address data.

The next four lines contain the same fields as the letter template created in the previous sections: Status, Name, Number and Street, Town and Postal Code, and Country. You could add another field for the post-box to the line with the house number and street if you wished.

Now skip three lines. The next two lines display all the business data in a row. Type these data as follows:

- Type 'Your Ref:' and press the Tab key twice.
- Type 'Your Letter Dated:' and press the Tab key.
- Type 'Our Ref:' and press the Tab key.
- Type 'Our Letter Dated:' and press Enter.
- Press Ctrl-F9 and type 'Your Ref' between the brackets.

In order to display the text in small letters, select the text and apply a 9 pts font size. Then place one field code on the next line. The other data relating to the standard layout on the previous line are filled from this field. Press Tab each time to move to the proper position under the relevant registration.

Skip two lines and enter the place and the date registration. To define the field for the PrintDate, open the *Insert* menu and select the *Field* option. Select the Date and Time category and select the PrintDate option from the Field Names list. Mark the whole line and give the commands to right-align the printdate. Restore left-alignment in the following line.

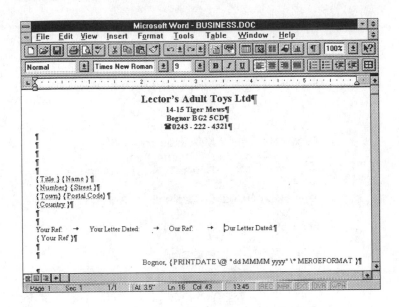

Save this document under the name BUSINESS. Just
for practice, print it once with the field codes and once
without.

You can use this document as the basis for a number
of letters. Save the adjusted version under a new name
each time so that the original structure is retained.
Keep in mind that the fields you skip on a line do not
occupy any space on the paper. For example, if you
skip the { Your Ref: } field and go on by pressing Tab to
the position under 'Your Letter Dated:' and type the appropriate date there, the date is then displayed neatly
in column 16 on the screen. However, the date is
shifted on the paper because { Your Ref: } has not
been used. Therefore it is always advisable to check
the layout in the Print Preview window prior to actually
printing the letter.
The problem of the unused fields can be solved by replacing these fields with an extra tab so that the rest of
the text remains correctly aligned on the paper as well.

Exercise 7b

Write a letter using the following data:

Sender	Lector's Adult Toys Ltd. 14-15 Tiger Mews Bognor BG2 5CD
Recipient	Mr. Gnasher Clark 69 Charnel Ave Dover DV3 4CD
Your Letter Dated	08 September 1994
Our Ref	Dream 17
Date	PrintDate
Contents	This letter is a reply to Mr. Clark's letter (DOLL.DOC) Mr. Lector offers his sympathy but regrets that he is unable to help due to the fact that the packing has been opened and Mr. Clark has attempted to repair any damage himself.

Check the letter using the Print Preview prior to saving it under the name REPLY.DOC. Then print the letter.

Answer 7b

The letter should look like the example shown below:

Lector's Adult Toys Ltd
14-15 Tiger Mews
Bognor BG2 5CD
Telephone 0243-222-4321

Mr. Gnasher Clark
69 Charnel Ave
Dover DV3 4HP

Your Ref: Your Letter Dated: Our Ref: Our Letter Dated:
            08 September 1994   Dream 17

                                    Bognor, 18 September 1994

Dear Mr. Clark,

I regret to inform you that **Lector's Adult Toys Ltd.** is
unable to help you in this matter. There are specific conditions of delivery which apply to all our mail order articles. These conditions are clearly shown in our catalogue. We are only able to accept any reclaim on articles
which are examined and proved to be defective on delivery.
In your case, you ought to have refused to accept the article in question.

Moreover, we regard your attempt to repair the article as
being rather inexpedient. The conditions of purchase
clearly state that the right to reclaim elapses when the
buyer makes alterations to the article delivered.

Accordingly, we hope to have reacted adequately to your
letter and expect to be of service to you in the future.

Yours Sincerely,

Supplements: The No-No Nanook Winter Look catalogue

```
 ═                          Microsoft Word - REPLY.DOC                    ▼ ▲
 ─  File  Edit  View  Insert  Format  Tools  Table  Window  Help          ▲
 [□][☞][🖫][🖨][🔍][✓] [✂][📋][📋][🖌] [↶±][↷±] [📄][📝] [▦][▧][⊞][◧][📊] [¶][100%][±][▶?]
 Normal        [±] Times New Roman [±] 10 [±] [B][I][U] [≡][≡][≡][≡] [≣][≣][⇥][⇤] [⊞]
 L ····1····¦····1····¦····2····¦····3····¦····1····¦····4····¦····1····¦····5····¦····1····↓ ▲
```

Lector's Adult Toys Ltd¶
14-15 Tiger Mews¶
Bognor B G2 5CD¶
☎ 0243 - 222 - 4321¶

¶
¶
¶
¶

{ Title } Mr { Name } G. Clark ¶
{ Number} 69 { Street } Charnel Street¶
{ Town} Dover { Postal Code} DV3 4HP ¶
{ Country }¶
¶
¶

Your Ref: →   Your Letter Dated: →   Our Ref: →   Our Letter Dated:¶
{ Your Ref } → 08 September 1994   →   Dream 17¶
¶
¶

Bognor, { PRINTDATE \@ "dd MMMM yyyy" * MERGEFORMAT }¶

```
 ▣◨⌨◄                                                                     ◄ ▶
 Page 1   Sec 1      1/1     At 3.7"   Ln 17  Col 40     13:57  REC  MRK  EXT  OVR  WPH
```

8 Advanced formatting techniques

There are various ways of assigning special layouts to texts so that they become more conspicuous or eye-catching. For example, you can place paragraphs in frames or at fixed positions surrounded by the rest of the text. Special characters can also be applied to give the text a different look.

8.1 Placing paragraphs in a frame

If you place a paragraph in a frame, this paragraph is emphasized in relation to the surrounding text. We shall illustrate this using the text shown below.

Example
Type the text shown below. Save it under the name SYSTEM.

                    System and Tactics

Tactics is more than a matter of deciding who is to
play where. It embraces a number of aspects involving the allocation of defensive and offensive tasks.
Defending does not only concern the prevention of
goals, it also comprises getting possession of the
ball in such a way that a team can switch to attack
as soon as possible. If you want to win, you have to
score.

Teams without tactics play like small children. They
swarm around the ball like rumours around Michael
Jackson. This bundle of energy produces a pinball
effect. The ball suddenly flies in one direction
followed by the entire bunch.

By positioning players more evenly over the field,
the ball can be played from one to the other. This
has various obvious advantages: the ball can move
faster than a player; the other team cannot score as
long as one has the ball. In addition, a team can
patiently build an attack which brings a player into
position to bombard the enemy goal. This player may
take risks, for if he loses the ball, most col-
leagues are still behind the ball and a counter attack need not be fatal.

Just as in all other team sports, systems and tactics in football have proved more effective in the
long run than individual skills. This does not mean
that the latter can be dispensed with. On the con-
trary, individualism is an essential part of all
team sport, not only bringing an element of surprise
when predictable manoeuvres fail, but also providing
entertainment for the spectators. The captivation
and enthralment of the spectators is every
promoter's dream. The big problem is: how does one
blend these three factors (effectiveness, individualism and entertainment) into a successful recipe?

There are almost as many different systems as there
are coaches. Nevertheless, there are broad tenden-
cies which can be concisely explained.

(From *Soccer for Dummies*)

The third paragraph deals with concrete application of
the subject matter and, accordingly, should be placed
in a frame to emphasize it. To do this, move the insertion point to the third paragraph and give the following
commands:

■   Open the *Format* menu.
■   Select the *Borders And Shading* option.
■   Select the Borders tab sheet if necessary.
■   Select the Shadow box in the Presets section.

- Select the 2¹/4 pt. line in the Line section.
- Press Enter or click on OK.

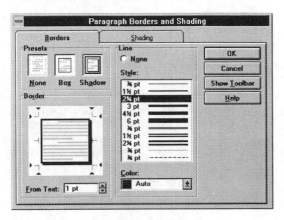

If you select the None option in the Presets section, this will remove a previously specified frame. The Frame option places a box around the entire paragraph and the Shading option we specified makes the right-hand and the bottom line of the frame thicker.
The thickness of the line is determined in the Line section. Under this, you can select a colour for the line ; this of course will only be displayed and printed if you have a colour monitor and printer.

In the Borders section, you can specify whether the lines are to be placed left, right, above and/or below the paragraph. When doing this, you first have to specify the position of the line and then the thickness of the line.

The distance between the frame and the text is normally 1 pt. You can change this by intervals of 1 pt. in the From Text box. The Show Toolbar button activates the Borders toolbar. The buttons on this toolbar enable you to apply frames to sections of text quickly and easily.

Defining lines

Example
The first paragraph of the SYSTEM text is to be assigned a line 3 pts thick next to the left margin.

This is done as follows:

■ First select the relevant passage of text.
■ Click on the Left Border button on the Borders toolbar (the button with the thick line at the left-hand side).
■ The Borders toolbar also contains buttons for defining various types of lines, borders and frames. The thickness of the line is determined in the options list at the left side of the toolbar.

Save the text under the name SYSTEM1.

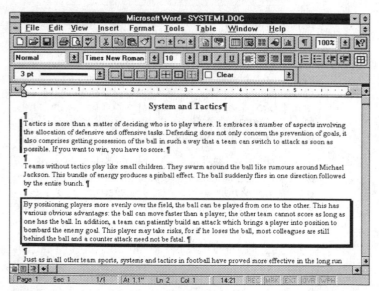

Shading

The Shading tab sheet in the Borders and Shading dialog window provides additional facilities for text layout.

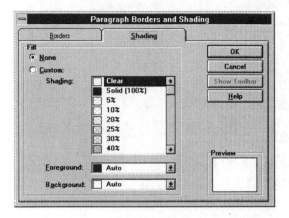

Example

We shall give the title a border with a line thickness of
1.5 pts and a shading with the pattern 25%. This is
done as follows:

- Select the title, System and Tactics
- Open the *Format* menu.
- Select *Borders and Shading*.
- Activate the Borders tab sheet.
- Select the 1$1/2$ pt line.
- Activate the Shading tab sheet.
- Click on 25%.
- Click on OK.

Save the document under the name SYSTEM2

The text will now look like this:

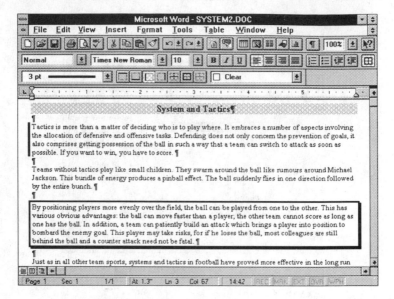

The exact nature of the shading on the paper depends on the printer being used. If you select a high shading percentage, it may occur that the text will become difficult to read. Shading without borders can be applied usefully in forms to mark positions where data have to be entered. If you have a colour printer at your disposal, you can create a special effect by choosing different colours for the foreground and background. You can only specify these settings in the Shading tab sheet of the Borders and Shading dialog box.

If you no longer need the Borders toolbar, you can deactivate it via the *Toolbar* option in the *View* menu. Or you can click on the Borders toolbar button at the extreme right of the Formatting toolbar .

8.2   Using frames

Anchoring paragraphs with the mouse

Anchoring a paragraph which has been placed in a frame is also a possibility to emphasize a particular aspect of the text. This technique is often used in advertising for instance; newspapers and magazines use it too to attract attention to certain topics. When working with Word, you can place text in a frame which can then be adjusted to your wishes. We shall illustrate this by means of the following text.

Example
Type the following text. Display the heading in boldface. Justify the text and activate the automatic hyphenation. Save the text under the name EMPLOYEE.DOC.

The ideal employee

Features which are not specific to the job, such as reliability and enthusiasm are highly esteemed by employers in interviews for jobs and apprenticeships.

Applicants who have completed school and apply for an apprenticeship appear to be able to compete with those who are older and more highly qualified. This is due to the fact that firms do not only take knowledge and experience into account but also character traits. In a recent survey, almost half of the employers consulted indicated that character is just as important as job-specific knowledge. An employee should be reliable, honest and enthusiastic and should show commitment to the function. The ideal employee shows initiative and is capable of finishing the job. Employers attach the least value to self confidence and stability.

The ideal employee is trustworthy and always available.

The last line (which is also the last paragraph) should now be placed in a frame in the middle of the second paragraph. To to this, a frame must first be placed around the text in question. Because this can be done quickly and easily using the mouse, we shall deal with this method first.

- Select the last paragraph.
- Click on the Bold button on the Formatting toolbar in order to make the characters bold.
- Open the *Insert* menu.
- Select the *Frame* option. A message box will inform you that the Page Layout View must be activated before you can see the frame. Acknowledge this by clicking on Yes.

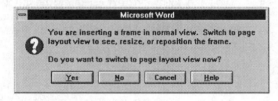

The paragraph is now displayed in a frame equipped with handles in the shape of small black squares.

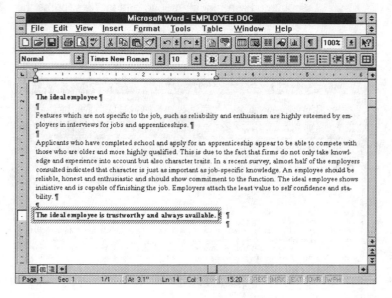

You can alter the size of the frame by placing the mouse pointer on one of these blocks and dragging it by holding down the left mouse button. As soon as the mouse pointer is placed on a handle, the arrow changes into a double-headed arrow which indicates the possible directions in which the frame can be enlarged or reduced.

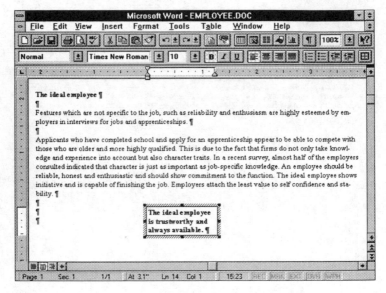

In order to decide on the best position for the text within the surrounding text, select the Page Width option from the Zoom Control list from the Standard toolbar (click on the arrow pointing downwards next to 100%). Use the mouse to move the framed paragraph to the middle of the second paragraph. This is done by placing the mouse pointer on the top of the frame *between* the handles. The mouse pointer assumes the shape of a normal selection arrow equipped with a four-headed black arrow. Now drag the frame to the middle of the second paragraph by holding down the left mouse button and releasing it when the paragraph is in the required position.

Revert to the 100% display once more.

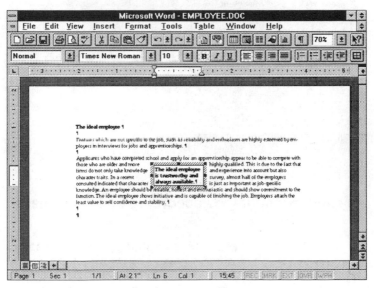

To improve the text layout, place the insertion point at the beginning of the paragraph and execute automatic hyphenation.

Save the text under the name EMPLOBOX.

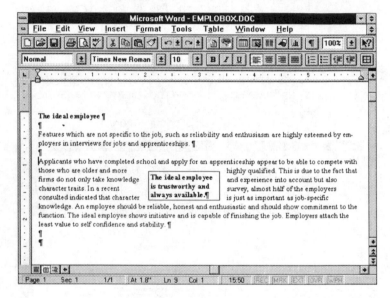

Anchoring paragraphs according to defined measurements

When you move a frame with the mouse, you do this according to what you see. The position is determined by estimating the relative proportions. We shall now specify the frame position in a more exact way.

Example
Place the insertion point in the frame and select the *Frame* option from the *Format* menu. The Frame dialog window displays the measurements and position of the frame. The various options in this dialog window enable you to alter these precisely to your requirements.

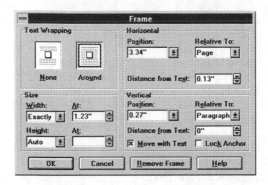

The Around option in the Text Wrapping section is selected, which means that the text will be placed around
the frame. The other option in this section, None, determines that the text will be placed above and below the
frame. The Size section enables you to specify the
Width and Height yourself or to have this done automatically.

The Horizontal section determines the position of the
frame in relation to the rest of the text. You can enter a
value here or select one of the standard positions.
Open the Horizontal Position drop-down list to see the
available options.

Left
The position is determined to the left of the orientation
point (Page, Margin or Column).

Right
The position is determined to the right of the orientation
point.

Center
The frame is placed exactly in the middle of the orientation point.

Inside
If the document is divided into left- and right-hand pages, you can use this option to determine that the frame is placed at the left-hand side of the orientation point on odd pages and at the right-hand side of the orientation point on even pages.

Outside
If this option is activated, the frame is always aligned to the outside of the page.

Distance from Text
The distance between the text and the frame is defined here.

It is also possible to specify your own values or to accept the standard options in the Vertical section. Open the drop-down list:

Top
Places the frame above the orientation point (Page, Margin or Paragraph).

Bottom
Places the frame under the orientation point.

Center
Places the frame in the middle of the selected orientation point.

It is possible to define the distance from the text here as well. If you activate the Move with Text option, the frame is moved along with the rest of the text when text is added or removed above or below the paragraph in the frame. The Lock Anchor option anchors the text in the paragraph to which it is linked.

Click on the Remove Frame button if you wish to remove the frame from the document.

8.3   Formatting documents in Page Layout view

The Page Layout view provides the facility of being able to check the document layout at any given moment, In addition, you can edit the margins and frames directly in this view. This is done by activating the horizontal and vertical ruler by means of the *Ruler* option from the *View* menu.

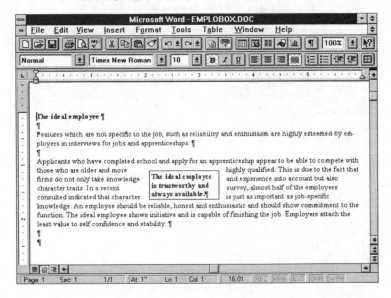

Place the mouse pointer between the two triangles on the horizontal ruler which are used for indentation. The mouse pointer then assumes the shape of a two-headed arrow. As soon as you press the left mouse button, the margin line appears in the document window. You can move this to the left or right by dragging it. If the insertion point is in a frame, thus making it active, you can alter the frame width in the same way. The height of the frame can also be altered in a similar manner using the vertical ruler.

Example

We shall illustrate this using the EMPLOYED document.

- Load the text and activate the Page Layout view.
- Open the *View* menu and select Ruler to display the rulers if they are not yet active.
- Move the left margin rightwards until the broken line reaches the left-hand side of the frame.
- Release the mouse button.

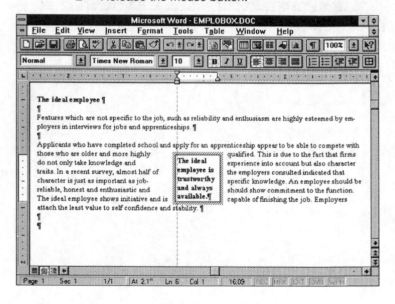

Save the document as EMPLOYD1.

Exercise 8

1   Load the EMPLOYEE text from the work diskette and place the heading in a double lined frame. Jot down the commands needed to do this.

_____
_____
_____
_____
_____
_____

Place a vertical line alongside the second paragraph. Jot down the commands needed to do this.

_____
_____
_____
_____
_____
_____

Save the text under the name EMPLOYD2.

2   Load the BUSINESS document. Place two folding
marks in the left margin of the letter. This is to be
done by typing a double hyphen in two new paragraphs at the end of the letter. Place both paragraphs in a frame.

Note down the commands needed to place the
folding marks. Specify the relevant values in the
Frame dialog window. Assuming the size of the
paper to be 11", the marks should be placed 3.6"
and 7.2" from the top edge.

_____
_____
_____

Width: _____ At: _____
Horizontal position: _____ Relative To: _____
Vertical position: _____ Distance from text: ____
_____ Relative To: _____
_____
_____
_____

Check the result in the Page Layout view and then
save the text under the name BUSIFOLD.

Answers 8

1   Load the EMPLOYEE text from the work diskette
    and place the heading in a double lined frame. Jot
    down the commands needed to do this.

    Select the title.
    Centre the title using the Centre button on the For-
    matting toolbar.
    Open the Format menu and select Borders and
    Shading.
    Select the Borders box and specify a double line
    ($1^{1}/2$ pt) in the Line section.
    Press Enter or click on OK.

    Place a vertical line alongside the second para-
    graph. Jot down the commands needed to do this.

    Select the lines in question.
    Open the Format menu and select the Borders
    and Shading option.
    In the Borders tabsheet, move to the Border sec-
    tion.
    Click on the middle symbol at the left-hand side.
    Select a single line in the Line section.
    Press Enter or click on OK.

Save the document under the name EMPLOYD2.

2   Load the BUSINESS text. Place two folding marks
    in the left margin of the letter. This is to be done by
    typing a double hyphen in two new paragraphs at
    the end of the letter. Place both paragraphs in a
    frame.

Note down the commands needed to place the folding marks. Specify the relevant values in the Frame dialog window. Assuming the size of the paper to be A4 (approx. 11"), the marks should be placed 3.6" and 7.2" from the top edge.

First type the double hyphens at the end of the document.
Select the first paragraph with the folding mark.
Open the Insert menu and select the Frame option.
You are asked if you wish to switch to the Page Layout View. Answer Yes.
Open the Format menu and select the Frame option.

Width: *Exactly*	At: *0.1"*
Horizontal position: *Left*	Relative To: *Page*
	Distance from text: *0.5*
Vertical position: *3.6"*	Relative To: *Page*

Click on OK or press Enter.
The frame is then removed by means of the following instructions:
Open the Format menu and select Borders and Shading.
Select the None option in the Presets section.
Click on OK.
Repeat the commands for the second folding mark. This time the vertical position is 7.2".

3   *If everything has gone smoothly, the Print Preview
    clearly shows the folding marks.*

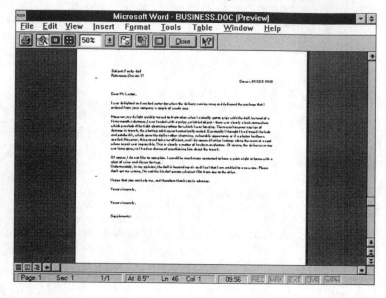

9   Search and Replace

When editing text, it often happens that you have to look for a special word. You may want to add something to the text at this point, but you may also wish to replace the word with another more suitable word.
This can be a very laborious and time-consuming task especially in lengthy texts. Fortunately Word has a function which can help you here: the search function. We shall outline how this works by means of the following text.

Example
Type the text shown below and save it under the name TRAIN.

Clothing makes the man

Seamus had to catch the early train. To be sure that he would sleep well, he had a good few doubles before settling down on the bench in the provincial railway station. As he took off his hat and coat to make himself comfortable, the stationmaster passed by. Seamus asked him if he would be sure to wake him at 5.30, just in time for the morning train. The stationmaster replied affirmatively. Moments later, a priest sat down beside Seamus and also made himself comfortable for the night. They exchanged a few words before Seamus, overpowered by drowsiness, fell into a deep sleep.

The next thing he knew, he was being vigorously shaken by the stationmaster. "Hurry up," he cried, "the train has arrived." Seamus got up, dressed quickly and ran to the train. He was rather surprised when the other passengers allowed him to step onto the train first, and how friendly everyone was. He moved through the corridor looking for an empty compartment where he could continue his sleep. Suddenly, he caught sight of himself in the mirror. To

```
his astonishment, he had the priest's hat and coat
on.

"That bloody fool of a stationmaster," he thought,
trying to suppress an upsurging rage, "he's woken
the wrong man!" Seamus rushed to the exit, got down
onto the platform and ran to the bench. It was
empty. Puzzled, he turned to see the train quietly
slip out of the station.
```

9.1   Searching for sections of text

We shall look for the word 'him' in the text. Of course, it
is quite easy to find it in the short text above but in
lengthy texts, as mentioned, this can be rather laborious.
Proceed as follows:

- Press Ctrl-Home to place the insertion point at the
  beginning of the text.
- Open the *Edit* menu.
- Select the *Find* command.
- Type the word 'him' in the Find What text box.
- Click on Find Next.

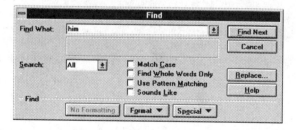

If you activate the Match Case option, the word will
only be sought in the specified style; in other words
'him' will be found but 'HIM' won't be. If you activate the
Find Whole Words Only option, the word will only be
found if it is a whole word; in other words, 'him' will be
found but 'himself' will not be.

When performing a search, you can make use of certain searching operators such as * and ?. Activate the Use Pattern Matching box if you want to use this function. For instance, if you specify the search word 'W???e, the program will find all words in a text which satisfy this criterion, such as 'Where', 'Whore', 'Write', 'While' etc. The question mark represents one missing character, an asterisk represents any number of missing characters. Thus, if you enter 'W*e' as the search word, the program would find all the words mentioned above and also words such as 'Woe' and 'Wiltshire'.

The Direct option enables you to specify the direction in which the search is to take place. You can specify Upwards (back towards the beginning), Downwards (to the end) or All (search the entire document). Normally the All option is the default setting. The Format button enables you to specify that the search action is to take the special format of characters and paragraphs into consideration. If you activate the No Format button, special formatting need not be taken into consideration in the search. If you click on the Special button, special characters in Word such as fixed spaces and tabs can be included in the search word.

9.2   Replacing sections of text

The TRAIN text contains the word 'doubles' at the beginning. We know Seamus and we also know that in his case it is much more likely to have been 'trebles'. Word has a function which can carry out substitution quickly and easily: Replace. This function is activated as follows:

- Press Ctrl-Home to move the insertion point to the beginning of the text.
- Open the *Edit* menu and select the *Replace* option.
- Type the word 'doubles' in the Find What box. This text can consist of a maximum of 255 characters.

- Type the word 'trebles' in the Replace With box. This text can also consist of a maximum of 255 characters.
- Activate the Replace button. The first occurrence of the sought word is replaced by the word specified in the Replace With box. You can replace all occurrences of a word, one by one, by clicking on the Replace button. As soon as the replace procedure has been concluded, this button ceases to be available. Quit the dialog box by pressing Esc or activating the Close button.

If you activate the Replace All button instead of the Replace button, the search word will be replaced throughout the text without any further confirmatory questions appearing.

Example

On second thoughts, the first version of the text was better. We shall replace 'trebles' with the original word 'doubles'. We shall also display original word in boldface. This is done as follows:

- Open the *Edit* menu and select *Replace*.
- Type the word 'trebles' in the Find What box.
- Type the word 'doubles' in the Replace With box.
- While the insertion point is still in the Replace With box, click on the Format button and then select the Font option.

■ Select Bold from the Font Style list on the Font tab
  sheet.
■ Click on the OK button.

The selected formatting feature appears under the Replace With text box in the Replace dialog box. You can
also specify a certain format for the text in the Search
For text box in a similar way.

■ Click successively on Replace, OK and Close.

Save the text under the name TRAIN.

If you perform a number of search and replace actions
in a session, the text boxes work as options lists in
which all search and replace words used in the session
have been included.

9.3 Using ANSI codes when search-
ing and replacing

Not all characters that can be placed on paper correspond to a character on the keyboard keys. Foreign letters with accents and tildes for instance are a good example. Nevertheless, these characters do occur on the
character lists used by the computer. Programs which
run under DOS use the ASCII table (American Standard Code for Information Interchange). The ANSI table (American National Standardization Institute), with
which Windows works, largely corresponds to the AS-
CII table.

You can produce all characters (including those which
have their own key on the keyboard) by typing their
codes in combination with the Alt key. Hold down the
Alt key and type the appropriate number on the *numeric keypad* at the right-hand side of the keyboard.
For instance, the key combination Alt-156 in ASCII will
produce a pound sign (£). In ANSI the key combination
Alt-0163 will produce the pound sign.

Appendix F presents the complete ANSI character set with the corresponding key combinations. Appendix G presents the ASCII table. In both tables, the codes 0 to 31 inclusive represent characters which cannot be shown on the screen. For instance, the number 13 belongs to the Enter key.

Typing texts containing many special characters is rather tedious. You have to remember the codes and then enter the corresponding codes by pressing four keys one by one. In cases like these, it is much easier to use temporary characters which you can use while typing the text and which can later be replaced by the correct character by means of the Search and Replace function.

For example, if you are writing a text with many financial pieces of information, you could simply type a backslash (\) instead of a pound sign (£). When you have completed the text, place the insertion point at the beginning of the text and open the *Edit* menu. Select the *Replace* option. Type the backslash in the Find What box and type Alt-0163 in the Replace With box. Then select the Replace All option. Word places the correct character throughout the text.

If you used for example the capital P instead of the backslash, you would have to activate the Whole Word option otherwise any word with a capital P would be assigned a pound sign throughout the text.

An even easier method is the AutoCorrect function in which characters are replaced during the actual typing.

9.4   AutoCorrect

The AutoCorrect function rectifies mistakes which frequently occur during typing. For example, the words 'hte' and 'cilck' are immediately converted to the proper words 'the' and 'click'. Special characters, from both the ANSI and the ASCII character sets can be automatically replaced in this way.

Example

Open the AutoCorrect dialog window by selecting this
option from the *Tools* menu.

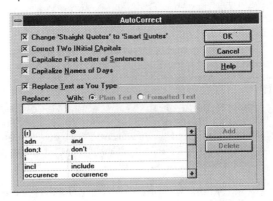

A number of fractions may already be defined in this
window. For instance, you only need to type a 1, a
slash and a 4 to get the program to transform this into
the 1/4 it should be. You can extend this list to provide
modifications to suit your own requirements.

We shall now enter the typing error 'hte' in the list and
have any occurrences automatically replaced by 'the'.

First type the erroneous spelling 'hte' in the Replace
text box. Then type the correct version in the With text
box. Activating the Add button will add the correction to
the alphabetical list.

This function is also convenient in texts where compli-
cated terms such as 'Methyl alcohol (CH_3OH)' and
'Ethyl alcohol (CH_3-CH_2OH)' can be temporarily replaced by terms such as 'BlindRot' and 'Gaga'.

In addition, frequently-used lengthy passages of text
can be adopted into the AutoCorrect list. For instance,
a lengthy passage about the benefits of the
Government's Income and Taxation Schemes can be

placed in the list. To do this, open the document with the relevant passage of text, select the passage in question and then select the *AutoCorrect* option from the *Tools* menu. Specify an appropriate abbreviation for the passage (such as GITS) for example.

The AutoCorrect also provides the possibility of replacing normal straight inverted commas with curled inverted commas.

Another handy feature of the AutoCorrect function is the removal of a second (erroneous) capital letter at the beginning of a word. In addition, you can ensure, by activating the relevant check box, that each sentence begins with a capital letter.

If you wish the corrections to actually be carried out during the typing process, activate the Replace Text During Typing option.

Example
Examine the following text. You will see a number of errors. Open the AutoCorrect window and type an erroneous word (or abbreviation) in the Replace box. Type the correct version in the With box. Click on the Add button. The word or abbreviation is added to the list.

```
The "AutoCorrect" function
```

```
By means of the AUtoCorrect function, you can have
words automatically corrected as you tyep. in this
way, the words are immediately transformed to the
proper version of the owrd. Special characters, from
both the ANSI and ASCII character sets, can be also
replaced bmo this function. This also applies to
special characters like (c) and 1/4, which can be
quickly and efficiently produced. The AUtoCorrect
function really improves the ease with which you can
work in Word. This is a splendd reason to purchase
the package asap.
```

If you now type the text as shown, AutoCorrect will correct the errors immediately. These words are stored for all future use. Activate all check boxes in the AutoCorrect dialog window. Type the following text, including the mistakes. Then save the text under the name CORRECT.

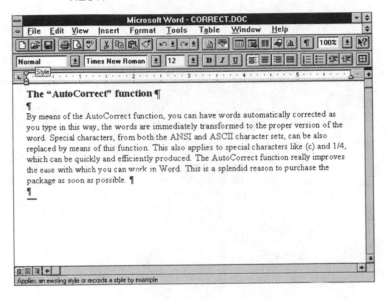

Exercise 9

1   In a text, you wish to carry out a check of all occurrences of the word 'Archaeopteryx'. You have a vague feeling that you might have ascribed the wrong dates to that period. Which commands are necessary to do this?

2   Add the abbreviations '5ds' and '3ds' to represent
    the terms 'five-and-a-quarter inch diskettes' and
    'three-and-a-half inch diskettes'.

    Type the following text about diskettes. The terms
    '360 Kb' etc. should have fixed spaces:

The following two types of diskettes are the most
common nowadays:

- **5ds:** diskettes with the specified diameter and a
capacity of 360 Kb or 1.2 Mb;

- **3ds:** diskettes with the specified diameter and a
capacity of 720 Kb or 1.44 Mb.

The 5 1/4 inch diskettes are generally used in older
types of personal computers (XTs).

The present generation of computers makes almost ex-
clusive use of diskdrives for 3 1/2 inch diskettes.

Answers 9

1   In a text, you wish to carry out a check of all occur-
    rences of the word 'Archaeopteryx'. You have a
    vague feeling that you might have ascribed the
    wrong dates to that period. Which commands are
    necessary to do this?

    Press Ctrl-Home to move the insertion point to the
    beginning of the text.
    Open the Edit menu and select Find.
    Type the search text 'Archaeopteryx' in the Find
    What text box.
    Click on Find Next.

2   Compare your text to the text below. If you experi-
    ment with moving the right margin a little to the left,
    you will see the effect of the fixed spaces.

```
The following two types of diskettes are
the most common nowadays:

- five-and-a-quarter inch diskettes: dis-
kettes with the specified diameter and a
capacity of 360 Kb or 1.2 Mb;

- three-and-a-half inch diskettes: dis-
kettes with the specified diameter and a
capacity of 720 Kb or 1.44 Mb.

The 5 1/4 inch diskettes are generally used
in older types of personal computers
(XTs).

The present generation of computers makes
almost exclusive use of diskdrives for
3 1/2 inch diskettes.
```

10 Headers, footers and footnotes

10.1 Adding page numbers

Page numbering is useful for documents which are longer than one page. They provide easy reference points for discussion.

The *Page Numbering* option is to be found in the *Insert* menu.

Example
Load the PRINMAR text. We shall add page numbering in Arabic numbers, centred at the bottom of the page. This is done as follows:

- Open the *Insert* menu.
- Select the *Page Numbers* option.
- Accept the default setting, Bottom of Page (footer).
- Select Center in the Alignment section.
- Press Enter or click on OK.

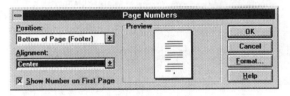

Save the text under the name PRINT4.

The Position options list provides, in addition to the default setting Bottom of Page, the possibility of placing the number as a header at the top of the page. Thus, the number is printed in the area that is reserved for headers and footers when the page margins are defined.

Normally, headers and footers are placed 0.5" from the edge of the paper, assuming that the top and bottom margins are wide enough. You can check the margin widths by selecting the *Page Setup* option from the *File* menu. Examine the Margins tab sheet.

If the margins are too narrow, the page numbers will not be printed. Keep this in mind if you are inserting single sheets of paper into the printer. Many printers reserve the first half inch for their own requirements, so that no page number will subsequently appear although you have taken the above information into account. In that case, you will have to increase the width of the margin(s).

The Number on First Page check box determines that the number should also be printed on the first page. The Format button enables you to specify which sort of number is to be placed. Word provides the following styles:

1 2 3 ...	Arabic numbers (standard)
a b c ...	Small letters
A B C ...	Capital letters
i ii iii ...	Roman numbers in small letters
I II III ...	Roman numbers in capital letters

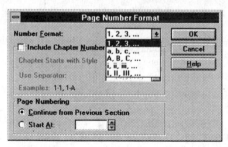

You can begin the page numbering with any chosen number. This is convenient when different sections or chapters of a book for example, have been saved as separate documents. To do this, specify the required number in the Start At box.

10.2   Headers and footers

Creating headers and footers

Example
We shall use the text about printers to illustrate how to add a header to both pages along with an integrated page number between hyphens. The header is to be centred.

- Load the document.
- Open the *View* menu.
- Select the *Header and Footer* option.
- Type 'Printer Info: page - '.

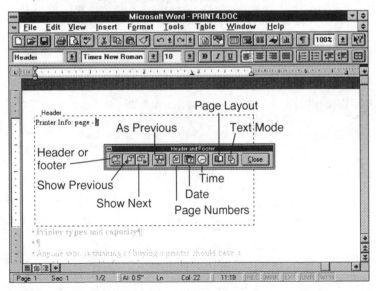

- Click on the Page Numbers button.
- Place a space with a hyphen.
- Centre the text by selecting it and clicking on the Center button on the Formatting toolbar.
- Click on Close.

Activate the Page Layout View to see the result. The header and the page number are displayed in the default font. If you wish to have a different font and/or font size, select the text in the Header section of the window and then choose the required features from the *Format* menu.

If the header or footer also has to be shown on the first page, or if you wish to place different headers and footers on the odd and the even pages, activate the relevant options in the Layout tab sheet of the Page Setup dialog box (via the *File* menu). The same result can also be gained by activating the buttons on the Header and Footer toolbar. The Show Previous and the Show Next buttons enable you to switch between the specified texts for these headers and footers. In this way, you can define three different headers and footers at one time.

Editing and removing headers and footers

In addition to the default settings for page numbering, date and time, you can also integrate a large number of field types in a header or footer.

Example
We shall include the file name in the header of the text about printers.
This is done as follows:
- Open the *View* menu.
- Select the *Header and Footer* option.
- Place the insertion point at the end of the header and then type four spaces.

- Open the *Insert* menu.
- Select the *Field* option.
- Select Document Information from the Categories options list.

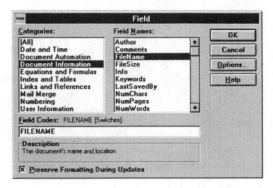

- Select the FileName option from the Field Names options list.
- Click on OK or press Enter. The name PRINT4 is adopted into the header.

Save the document under the name PRINT4.

If you wish to edit the file name when the document has been saved, select the *Header and Footer* option from the *View* menu. Move the insertion point to the field. Press F9 to edit the file name. As soon as you close the file, as message box appears asking if you wish to save the changes. The changes are only saved if you answer Yes to this question.

When you select the field, you can open a shortcut menu by pressing the right mouse button. This menu contains the *Update Field* and *Toggle Field Codes* options.

Headers and footers can be removed from a text by selecting their contents and pressing Del.

10.3 Footnotes

Creating footnotes

Remarks and notes which are important enough to be added to text but not important enough to interrupt the continuity of the text are often placed in footnotes at the bottom of the page. Do not confuse these with footers which contains standard text and are placed at the bottom of every page.

Footnotes have an important function in providing supplementary information and acknowledgements and references, especially in scientific publications.

Example
We shall outline how to work with footnotes by means of a text fragment from Hamlet, perhaps the best-known of all Shakespeare's plays.
When we have typed the text, we shall add a footnote to make a comment on the text.

Type the text shown below and save it under the name LOST.

```
"To be, or not to be: that is the question:
Whether 'tis nobler in the mind to suffer
The slings and arrows of outrageous fortune,
Or to take arms against a sea of troubles,
And by opposing end them? To die: to sleep;
No more; and, by a sleep to say we end
The heart-ache and the thousand natural shocks
That flesh is heir to, 'tis a consummation
Devoutly to be wished. To die, to sleep;
To sleep: perchance to dream: ay, there's the rub;
For in that sleep of death what dreams may come
When we have shuffled off this mortal coil,
Must give us pause."
```

- Place the insertion point immediately behind the word 'them'. Ensure that the Page Layout View is *not active*.
- Open the *Insert* menu.
- Select the *Footnote* option.
- Click on OK or press Enter.

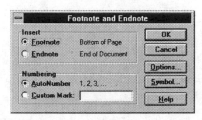

The Footnote option is automatically activated in the Insert section. This default setting displays footnotes at the bottom of the page. If you like, you can activate the Endnote option which will place the footnote at the end of the document. This is very common in scientific articles.

The Automatic Numbering in the Numbering section is normally active so that the numbering of the footnotes is automatically carried out. As soon as you add or remove a footnote, the numbering is adjusted. The Custom Marks option enables you to specify a symbol for the footnotes yourself. The Symbol button opens a list of available characters (Symbols or Wingdings).

The Options button opens the Note Options dialog window, providing the All Footnotes and All Endnotes tab sheets. The Place At list enables you to group the footnotes or endnotes together at the end of a section, for instance, or at the end of the entire document.
In the Numbering section you can specify whether you wish to have continuous numbering or numbering which begins anew at each new section.

When you have confirmed the settings in the Footnote and Endnote dialog window, a small Footnote window will appear showing the selected footnote character. This character is also located in the text section where the footnote is to be placed. Type the footnote in this small window.

In our case, the footnote text will be as follows:

```
It would appear evident that Hamlet at this
point acknowledges that there is no hope of re-
covery. The fight against the circumstances is
already lost; death is the only solution to the
sea of troubles. He is retreating into his own
perceptions.
```

When doing this, keep the following in mind:

- When typing, ensure that coherent passages of text are linked by fixed spaces and fixed hyphens.
- In the small Footnote window, the default font is used in the 10 pts size. If you wish to alter this, select the footnote and change the format using the options from the *Format* menu.
- Format the footnotes using the options in the Paragraph dialog window (*Format* menu) in such a way that the footnotes have a left indentation and the text is left-aligned.

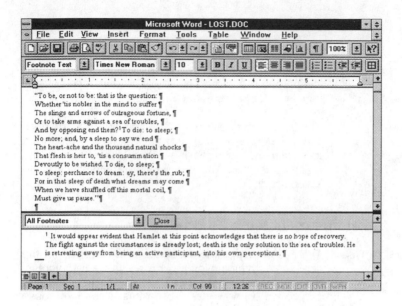

Via the options list in the Footnote window, you can specify whether the footnotes or the footnote separators are to be displayed. The window is closed by clicking on the Close button. To continue editing the text, press F6 to return to the document itself. Pressing the same key again will return you to the Footnote window to edit a footnote if required. The footnote character is automatically displayed in superscript.

In the Page Layout View, the footnote is automatically shown at the required position on the page once you have closed the Footnote and Endnote dialog window. You can then type the footnote. You can place the insertion point at the footnote by means of the Go To command.

Removing a footnote

If you wish to remove a footnote, select the footnote indication character (in this case, the character behind
'them') and press the Del key. The numbering of any
remaining footnotes is automatically adjusted.

If you unintentionally remove a footnote, this deletion
can be undone by selecting the *Undo* command from
the *Edit* menu or by clicking on the Undo button on the
Standard toolbar. The numbering is automatically adjusted again.

Altering the Footnote window

The Footnote window occupies a lot of space on the
screen. When typing lengthy texts with many footnotes,
this can be rather disturbing. However, it is possible to
reduce the window size. To do this, place the mouse
pointer on the separating line between the document
window and the Footnote window. Then drag the line
downwards to the required position. The Footnote window is then closed by clicking on the Close button or by
selecting the *Footnote* option from the *View* menu. The
Footnote window can be opened again by selecting the
same option once again.

In the Page Layout View, you can directly edit the footnotes which are situated at the bottom of the page.
Place the insertion point at the footnotes. In the case of
lengthy texts with many footnotes, you can use the *Go
To* function from the *Edit* menu to switch to a certain
footnote. The insertion point is moved to the required
footnote as follows:

- Open the *Edit* menu.
- Select the *Go To* option.
- Select the Footnote option from the Go To What
  list.
- Type the number of the required footnote in the
  Enter Footnote Number box.

- Click on the Go To button.
- Click on the Close button.

Exercise 10

1 You have prepared a lecture. The text is stored on disk in the computer. You wish to add the following footnote:

Lecture: 10th of August 1994 - Survival - page {PAG}

Which commands do you need to give?

_____

_____

_____

_____

_____

_____

_____

_____

2 Load the HAMLET text and add the following text:

Unlike the great Greek tragedies, Shakespeare empha-
sised not only the insignificance of the individual
in the cosmic wheel of fortune, he also accentuated
the dichotomy within the individual himself; the
protagonist is divided into the dubious and sometimes untenable combination of body and spirit. This
awareness of 'lostness' became an increasingly important theme in literature in subsequent centuries
and perhaps reached its climax in the literary work
of the French 'existentialists' like Sartre and Camus in the 20th century.

Note down the commands necessary to create a footnote at the bottom of the page.

There should be references to works of Sartre and Camus in two footnotes, as follows:

see esp. J.P. Sartre *La Nausée* (1938)

and

see esp. A. Camus *L'Etranger* (1942)

Print the text and save it under the name ALL-LOST.

Answers 10

1   You have prepared a lecture. The text is stored on
     disk in the computer. You wish to add the following
     footnote:

Lecture: 10th of August 1994 - Survival - page {PAG}

Which commands do you need to give?

Open the View menu and select the Header and
Footer option.
Click on the Header or Footer and then on the
Header/Footer button (extreme left of the toolbar)
to switch to the footer.
Type 'Lecture: 10th of August - Survival - page
{PAG}'.
Click on the Page Numbering button on the
Header and Footer toolbar.
Close the window by clicking on the Close button.

2   Load the HAMLET text and add the text as given
     above.

     Note down the commands necessary to create a
     footnote at the bottom of the page.

     Open the Insert menu.
     Select the Footnote option.
     Press Enter or click on OK.

When the footnotes have been added at the appropriate places, the Print Preview of the text should look like this:

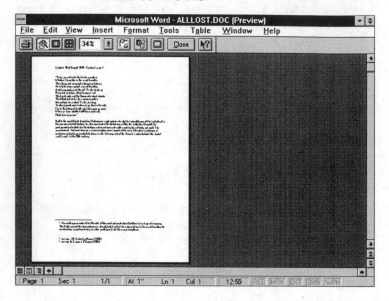

11 Using Tabs

11.1 Creating an Invoice template

Simple use of tab stops can make a document much more attractive. We shall discuss this topic in the light of creating a template for an invoice. The figure below displays a template for Lector's Adult Toys Ltd. which has been created using tabs. We shall use some of the headings in the REPLY.DOC document for this example.

Lector's Adult Toys Ltd
14-15 Tiger Mews
Bognor BG2 5CD
☎ 0243-222-4321

```
deb. nr:  0001
invce. nr: 0001


                                      Bognor, 0 XXX 0000

                         INVOICE

------------------------------------------------------------
art nr   quantity   description   price per art.      sum
------------------------------------------------------------



                                              - - - - - - - - -


VAT 17.5%
                                              - - - - - - - - -

TOTAL SUM
                                              =========

Yours Sincerely,
```

The letter heading, the area containing the address data of the recipient, the place and date registration have remained the same. The page layout and the character formatting are also identical.

The lines with references have been replaced with data which are important on an invoice. The fields where the debit number and the invoice number have to be entered are placed behind a tab.

In order to get a good look at the effects of placing tab stops, the Ruler should be activated. Normally Word places a tab stop every 0.5". This is not very handy for an invoice because it contains columns of unequal width. In Word, tab stops are linked to paragraph marks so that we can apply deviating tab stops in the invoice section.

Creating the invoice section

Before combining the invoice and the letter template, we shall first create the invoice section in a new document. Open the *File* menu, select *New* and confirm the Normal settings (Descriptions shows Default Document Template).

The invoice section is to begin with the debit number and the invoice number. Type 'deb. nr:' and press the Tab key. Then press Ctrl-F9 to place a field at this position.
Press Cursor Right to move out of the field and type 'invce. nr:'. Press Tab and Ctrl-F9 again.

Create two blank lines and type the word 'INVOICE' in a 12 points font size and in capitals. Select it and click on the Center button on the Formatting toolbar.
This is followed by a blank line. Select left-alignment again and select a 10 pts font size. Type a line full of hyphens. Shift the text in the document window upwards using the mouse and scroll bar so that the line on which the reference numbers such as 'art. nr.' etc.

are to be placed are immediately under the Ruler. Now type 'art. nr.'. The insertion point is approximately 0.4" from the left margin. The first tab stop in this paragraph should therefore be a little further over on the paper, at 0.8" for example. To specify this, open the *Format* menu and select *Tabs*.

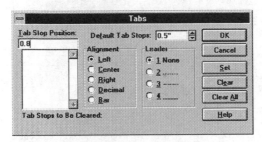

At Tab Position type '0.8'. You can accept the other settings. The tab stop is to be left-aligned and we shall not use any leading characters. If you then click on the Set button, the tab stop will be placed but the dialog window will remain open so that you can place more tab stops. When you choose OK, the tab stop is set and you will return to the document window.

We shall place the other tab stops at the required positions in the same way.

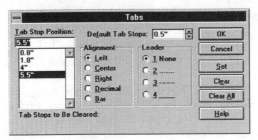

Type the subheadings, 'quantity', 'description', 'price per art.' and 'sum'.

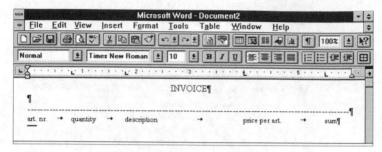

The paragraph for the invoice itself is placed under a second dividing line. This paragraph deviates from the previous one because a different tab stop is used for the amounts. In the Tabs dialog window, you can select one of four different sorts of tabs. The distinction is shown in the figure below.

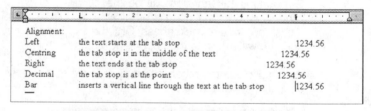

Because tab stops apply to an entire paragraph, we only need to format one line to create the template.

The invoice is completed with four paragraphs, in other words, press Enter 4 times to create space for future entries. To add up the amounts, a new paragraph is opened with approximately ten right-aligned hyphens. Click on the right-alignment button and type the hyphens. Similarly, we place a stripe three lines lower for the second addition sum and then, two lines lower, a number of equals signs to complete the structure.

The paragraph with the subtotal and the VAT only needs one tab stop at 5.75", aligned to the decimal point. This also applies to the paragraph with the invoice sum.

Save the document as INVOICE.DOC. The result will now be as follows:

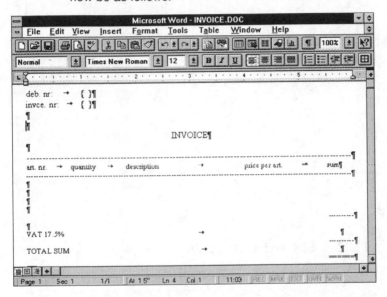

The tab stops are displayed here in the document window with arrows pointing to the right.

Example
Open a new document and create the invoice section of the template. Define an empty field behind 'deb. nr.', 'inv. nr.', at the subtotal, at 'VAT' and at 'TOTAL SUM'.

The result should be as follows:

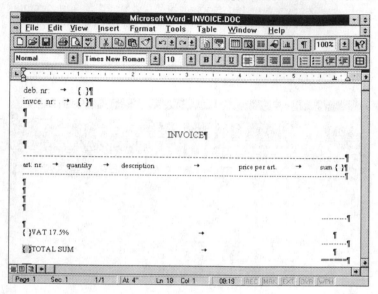

11.2   Using windows

The INVOICE.DOC document is not quite ready for
use. The letter heading and the address fields still have
to be placed above the invoice, and a footer containing
the bank account number has to be placed under the
invoice. We shall make use of the possibility in Word of
working with several texts at once. While the IN-
VOICE.DOC text is still on the screen, we open the RE-
PLY text. This is automatically loaded into a second
window. You can switch back and forward between the
texts by means of the *Window* menu.

When you open this menu, you can activate another window by clicking on the name or typing the number shown in front of it.

We shall import the letter heading from the REPLY document into the INVOICE.DOC document. This is done as follows:

■ Open the *Window* menu and select the REPLY document.
■ Place the insertion point at the beginning of the REPLY document by pressing Ctrl-Home.

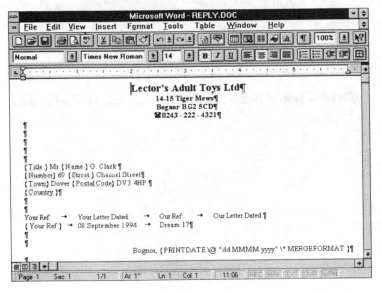

■ Select the letter heading and the address fields using the mouse or by pressing F8 and the cursor keys.
■ Copy the selection to the Clipboard using the *Copy* command from the *Edit* menu.
■ Open the *Window* menu and activate the IN-VOICE.DOC document.

- Place the insertion point at the beginning of the document by pressing Ctrl-Home.
- Select the *Paste* command from the *Edit* menu.

Return to the REPLY document by selecting it from the *Window* menu. Select the place and date registration by pressing F8 or using the mouse. Make sure you select the entire line including the paragraph mark. This ensures that the alignment is also copied.

Now copy this registration to the INVOICE document by selecting *Copy* from the *Edit* menu, switching to the INVOICE document, placing the insertion point at the required position and choosing *Paste* from the *Edit* menu.

If you now examine the field codes (*Tools* menu, *Options*, Field Codes), your document will look like this:

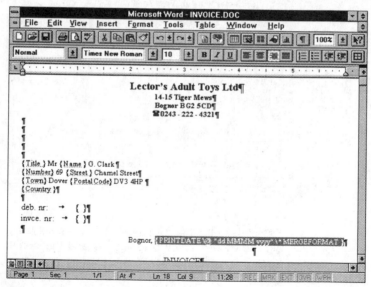

We shall now create a footer containing the following data.

```
Bank Account Number: Bank of England 123456789098765
Please state debit and invoice number
```

The footer is placed as follows:

- Open the *View* menu and select *Header and Footer*.
- Switch to the Footer window if necessary by clicking on the Header/Footer button (extreme left on the Header and Footer toolbar).
- Type the above lines in the Footer window.

Close the Footer window and save the document under the name INVOICE2.

11.3   Using tab stops

Example
Using the INVOICE2 template, we shall type an invoice containing the following data:

```
debitor     Mr. Gnasher Clark
            69 Charnel Ave
            Dover DV3 4HP

debit nr:   1234
invce nr:   5678

date: will be placed in the document automatically
```

Mr. Clark has made two mail orders, one consisting of four brown rabbits (article number 2134) costing £13.45 each, and a talking foot massage device (article 5656) costing £98.50.

The invoice is created by pressing the Cursor Right, Tab or F11 keys to place the data shown above at the appropriate positions. The invoice should then resemble the figure below.

Save the document under the name GNASHER2 and print it.

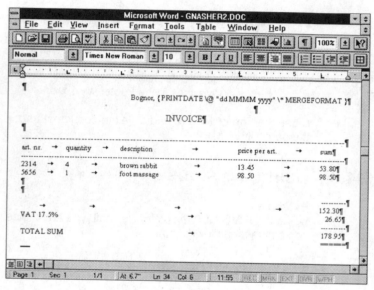

The invoice should resemble that shown below. Depending on the connected printer, your example may differ slightly from the one here. In that case, you may have to make small adjustments if you wish to make them identical.

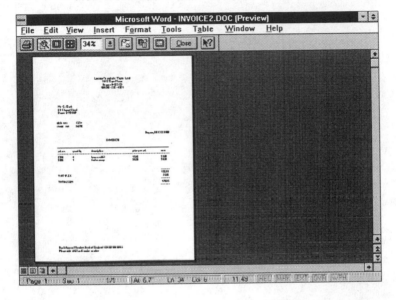

Lector's Adult Toys Ltd
14-15 Tiger Mews
Bognor BG2 5CD
☎ 0243-222-4321

```
Mr. Clark
69 Charnel Ave
Dover DV3 4HP


debit nr:  1234
invce. nr: 5678
```

                                                   Bognor, 23 Sept 1994

                                 INVOICE

```
---------------------------------------------------------------
art nr    quantity  description     price per art.            sum
---------------------------------------------------------------
2134         4      brown rabbit        13.45              53,80
5656         1      foot massage        98.50              98.50
                                                        ---------
                                                          152.30
VAT 171/2 %                                                26.65
                                                        ---------
TOTAL SUM                                                 178,95
                                                        =========
```

```
Bank Account Number: Bank of England 123456789098765
Please state debit and invoice number
```

11.4   Altering and deleting tab stops

We shall now demonstrate how to alter and remove tab stops, using the GNASHER2 document. We shall alter the tab used to move to the article description. This will become a tab for centring text. We shall also use dots as leading characters. To do this, place the insertion point in the line containing the first article and give the following commands:

- Open the *Format* menu.
- Select the *Tabs* option.
- Select the tab at 1.8" from the Tab Position list. Then click on the Clear button.
- In the Tab Stop Position box, type 2.5" to place a new tab stop.
- Select the Center option from the Alignment section.
- Select option 2 from the Leader section.
- Click on the Set button.
- Click on OK.

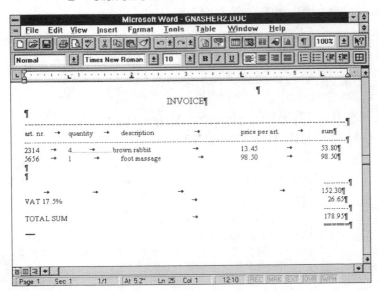

If you are not completely satisfied with the result, you can restore the previous situation by means of the *Undo* option from the *Edit* menu.

11.5   Deleting all tab stops in a paragraph

Example
As an example, we shall remove all the tab stops in the GNASHER2 invoice in the section listing the articles sold. Make sure that you have saved the document on the work diskette so that you will not lose it if anything goes wrong.

Proceed as follows to remove all the tabs:

- Select the appropriate section.
- Open the *Format* menu.
- Select the *Tabs* option.
- Click on the Clear All button.
- Press Enter or click on OK.

Caution: The tabs will be deleted without any safe-guard question.

Only the default settings remain.

11.6   Setting and moving tab stops using the mouse

You can also set tabs using the mouse. To illustrate this, we shall set the tabs which we have just removed back into the document. Setting tabs at exact positions using the mouse is a bit tricky. The most simple way is to place the line which is to receive the new tab settings exactly under the Ruler. Then place the insertion point in the paragraph or section in question (the tabs are linked to the paragraph marks).

Left-aligned, centred, right-aligned, decimal

At the extreme left-hand side of the Ruler, you will see one of the four symbols for left- and right-aligned, and centred and decimal tab stops. At the moment, this looks a bit like a capital **L**. The active type of tab stop is changed by clicking on this box. You can then set a tab stop of the selected type by clicking on the required position on the Ruler. The entire procedure is as follows:

■ Place the insertion point in the paragraph in which the tab stop is to be active.
■ Click on the box at the left-hand side of the Ruler until the required tab stop becomes active.
■ Click with the left mouse button on the position on the Ruler where the tab stop is to be placed. A vertical broken line appears on the screen indicating the tab stop position in the document.

As long as you hold down the mouse button you can alter the tab position by dragging the mouse. If you double click on the left mouse button, the Tabs dialog window is opened.

Exercise 11

1   Which commands are necessary to remove all the tab stops in a paragraph or selected section?

2   Create an introduction for the SYSTEM text. Do this by copying the first paragraph of the SOCCER text. Save the text under the name GAME.

Answers 11

1   Which commands are necessary to remove all the
    tab stops in a paragraph or selected section.

    Place the insertion point in the paragraph or select
    the appropriate section of text.
    Open the Format menu and select Tabs.
    Click on the Clear All button.
    Press Enter or click on OK.

2   Create an introduction for the SYSTEM text. Do
    this by copying the first paragraph of the SOCCER
    text. Save the text under the name GAME.

    Proceed as follows:
    Open the File menu and select New.
    Confirm the Normal template for a document.
    Load the SYSTEM text.
    Load the SOCCER text.
    Select the first three paragraphs of the SOCCER
    text.
    Open the Edit menu and select Copy.
    Open the Window menu and select the SYSTEM.
    Press Ctrl-Home to ensure that the insertion point
    is at the beginning of the document.
    Open the Edit menu and select Paste.
    Select Save As from the File menu.
    Save the new document under the name
    GAME.DOC

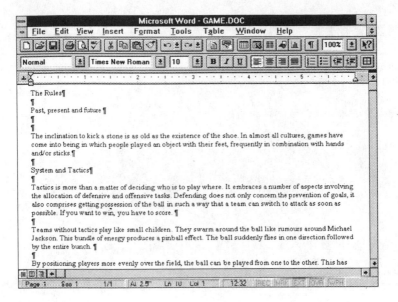

The Rules¶
¶
Past, present and future ¶
¶
¶
The inclination to kick a stone is as old as the existence of the shoe. In almost all cultures, games have come into being in which people played an object with their feet, frequently in combination with hands and/or sticks.¶
¶
System and Tactics¶
¶
Tactics is more than a matter of deciding who is to play where. It embraces a number of aspects involving the allocation of defensive and offensive tasks. Defending does not only concern the prevention of goals, it also comprises getting possession of the ball in such a way that a team can switch to attack as soon as possible. If you want to win, you have to score. ¶
¶
Teams without tactics play like small children. They swarm around the ball like rumours around Michael Jackson. This bundle of energy produces a pinball effect. The ball suddenly flies in one direction followed by the entire bunch. ¶
¶
By positioning players more evenly over the field, the ball can be played from one to the other. This has

12   AutoText: Working with fragments of text

12.1   Creating a special template for fragments of text

Unless otherwise specified, all texts which are newly created in Word are based on the NORMAL.DOT template which produces the standard layout. This is responsible for paragraph alignment and the default font, among other things. If you frequently work with a certain structure (fonts, font sizes, fields etc.) which differ from the standard structure, you may wish to make your own adapted structure the standard one so that you do not continually have to make adjustments to the default settings each time you create a new document.

However, if other people also work with your computer, any alterations to the standard template may cause problems for them. Therefore, it is advisable to create a separate template which fulfils your requirements and which can be activated each time you wish to create a new document.

In this chapter, we shall create a template which will incorporate text fragments which we frequently use.

Proceed as follows in order to ensure that there is a separate template available for test fragments:

- Close all files.
- Open the *File* menu.
- Select *New*.
- Click on the Template option button in the New section in the subsequent dialog box. Instead of a new document, a new template will be opened.
- Click on OK. The familiar screen reappears. However, 'Template1' is shown on the title bar, indicating that a new template is to be edited. All settings

of the NORMAL.DOT template will also be adopted initially.

■ Open the *File* menu.

■ Select the *Save As* option.

■ Type the file name *a:newtempl* or a name of your choice. The extension DOT is automatically added. The Newtempl template will now be saved on the diskette in drive A:.

In this template we shall save the fragments of text which we often make use of. And when creating new documents we can activate this NEWTEMPL template instead of the Normal template.

We shall now create a new document. Accordingly, select the *New* command from the *File* menu and type *A:\Newtempl* in the Template text box or choose it from the list.

The text fragments can now be created.

12.2   Text fragments

A good word processor like Word, provides the facility of recording this passage just once and saving it under its own name as a fragment which can be quickly and easily inserted into a document. These standard passages are frequently used in business letters for instance. If you make use of text fragments, quotations and invoices for example no longer need to be conceived and typed every time; they can be compiled out of the appropriate text fragments. Text fragments are also convenient in a different area. It is much easier to have ready-made replacements for abbreviations in your text. It is much easier for a chemical engineer to type 'pvc' than 'polyvinylchloride' for example.

In this chapter, we shall discuss the usage of text fragments when dealing with address data and creating letters.

12.3   Creating the text fragments

For the first text fragment, type the address data in boldface, centred, as shown in the figure below. Separate the lines using Shift-Enter, so that the text fragment can also be used in the following chapter which deals with form letters.

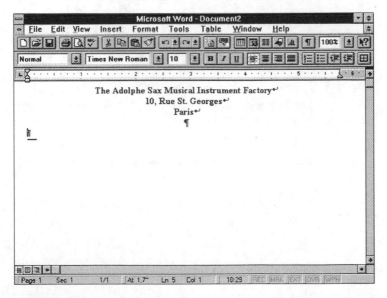

Proceed as follows to save the text as a text fragment:

- Select the entire text fragment.
- Open the *Edit* menu.
- Select the *AutoText* option.
- Enter the name 'Sax Instr. Factory' in the Name section.
- Make the text fragments available to *only the documents which are based on the NewTempl template* by selecting this from the template options list (Make AutoText Entry Available To).
- Click on the Add button.
- Press the Del key to delete the selected text.

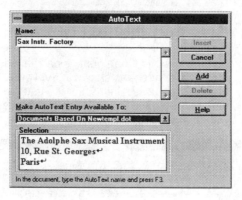

The first address (the heading) is now saved as a text fragment in working memory.

Example
We shall enter the following address data as text fragments.

```
Mr. Arnett Cobb
21 Timeless Drive
Cobham CH2 4CD
```

```
Mr J. Coltrane
444 Sonny Rd
Colchester CL2 4FG

Mr D. Gordon
2 Power Towers
Gorlington GL3 3GH

Mr C. Hawkins
5 Desafinado Ave
Hawthorn HW2 1TH

Mr B. Marsalis
6 Bloomington Bridges
Marchmont MM2 8EH
```

Enter these addresses, left-aligned, in the same way as shown above for the instrument manufacturing company. Conclude each line by pressing Shift-Enter.

The name of the text fragment may consist of a maximum of 32 characters. You can link words together into one word by typing the underlining character between the words. The text fragment may occupy a page or more, but if that is the case it is rather exaggerated to save it as a mere text fragment.

Formatting features can be included in the text fragment just as in normal texts. When formatting paragraphs, you have to pay attention to the fact that the format is only adopted if the paragraph mark is part of the text fragment. If that is not the case, the paragraph formatting is not applied to the text fragment.

12.4   Saving and loading text fragments

In order to make the above text fragments available for future texts when you start up Word, the Newtempl template on the diskette has to be brought up to date. When you quit Word or close NEWTEMPL.DOT, a

message window appears on the screen, asking if you
wish to save any alterations to this template. Reply Yes
to save the text fragments in the NEWTEMPL.DOT.
This ensures that the next time you open Word, you
can also use the text fragments.

12.5   Inserting text fragments

To illustrate how to insert text fragments, we shall write
a letter to Mr. J. Coltrane using the letter heading we
shall create for Adolphe Sax, Instrument Maker Ltd. In
the letter we shall ask Mr. Coltrane whether he would
like to examine some new instruments. In this letter we
shall suggest making an appointment.

Example
Open a new document and type *a:\newtempl* in the
Template box. This gives you access to the text frag-
ments which you saved earlier.

Open the *Edit* menu and select *AutoText*. The names
of the fragments available are shown in the list. Select
the heading, 'Sax Instr. Factory' and click on the Insert
button. The text is immediately imported into the new
document.

Leave a blank line under the address. The cursor is
now in line 5 (see Status line at the bottom of the
screen). As in previous letters, we should place the address at a position which will correspond to the window
of a window envelope.
Move to line 8 by pressing Enter. Now press Ctrl-F9 to
place a field here. Type 'address' between the field
braces and hide the text by selecting it (press F8 twice)
and pressing Ctrl-Shift-H.

Save these blank lines and the 'address field' by selecting them, opening the *Edit* menu and typing a name
in the text box, 'address field'. Click on the Add button.
This means that in future documents you can enter the

right amount of empty space in your letter by selecting this piece of AutoText. The hidden field ensures that only the address which you subsequently insert will be printed and not the field itself.

Move the insertion point to just behind the address field.

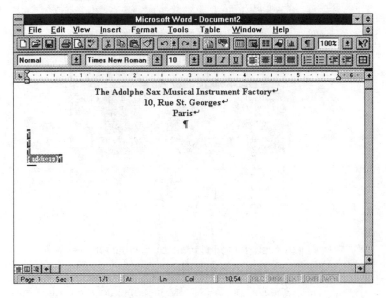

You can insert the text fragment in two ways:

Method 1:

- Place the insertion point behind the { address } field.
- Type the name of the fragment in this case, Coltrane.

- Press F3 or click on the Insert button (13th from the left on the Standard toolbar).

Method 2:

- Place the insertion point behind the { address } field.
- Open the *Edit* menu.
- Select the *AutoText* option.
- Type 'Coltrane' or select the name from the list.
- Click on Insert.

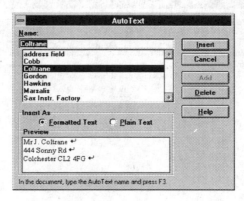

Summarising, the full procedure is as follows:

- Open the *File* menu and choose *New*.
- Specify the NEWTEMPL template from the Template list (or *a:\newtempl* if you have it on diskette).
- Click on OK.
- In the new document, place the insertion point at the position where you wish the text to come.
- Open the *Edit* menu and select *AutoText*.
- Select the name of the required text from the list.
- Click on the Insert button.

The character formatting features which are saved along with the text fragments are automatically applied. If you wish to insert a text fragment without these features, select the Plain Text option in the Insert As section of the AutoText dialog box.

Example

We shall create a template for Adolphe Sax. Then we shall insert Mr Coltrane's address this letter template. Complete the letter using the following text and save it under the name APPOINT1.

```
Dear Sir,

The Sax Instrument company is again on the verge of
a revolutionary musical invention. Taking advantage
of modern technology, we have now been able to place
an electronic sensor in the body of the saxophone.
This sensor, which can be programmed in different
ways, reacts to rapid movements of the
instrumentalist's eyes, eyelids, or other close-
range objects. The settings, geared to the specified
object (eye, eyelid) can be used to create, swell or
distort the upper or lower flageolet tones or to
create any particular (dis)harmony. Rhythmic pulses
based on the movement of eyes or eyelids are also
possible. The great advantage is that, unlike a
synthesizer, the tones produced are the real acous-
tic saxophone tones you produce yourself. We imagine
that this invention may be of some interest to you
as one of the leading present day exponents of the
instrument.
Accordingly, we invite you to participate in our
elite workshop and to give your opinion of the new
technological developments. This will take place on:

                            Friday 11th November 2 p.m.

Yours Sincerely,
```

This is done as follows:

- Begin a new document based on the Newtempl template.
- Insert the text fragments at the appropriate positions (heading, address etc.)

- Type the place, and insert a field for the date. This is done by opening the *Insert* menu and selecting *Field*. Click on Date and Time in the Categories section and then on PrintDate in the Field Names section.
- Subsequently click on OK.
- Type the text as shown.

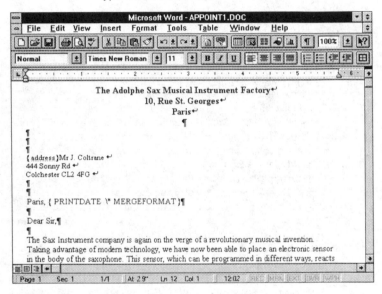

Making use of existing structures

You may wish to make use of existing structures in existing documents. You may wish to add fragments of text from other templates. In that case, the new template should be linked to the document with the required structure or information.

Example

We shall load the REPLY.DOC which was created using the NORMAL.DOT template. Subsequently, we shall link the NEWTEMPL template to the document in memory so that we can make use of the text fragments stored there.

The link between the REPLY document and the text fragments in the NEWTEMPL template is made as follows:

- First load the REPLY.DOC.
- Open the *File* menu.
- Select the *Templates* option.
- Click on the Add button.
- Select drive A.
- Select the file name NEWTEMPL.DOT
- Click on OK. The Add Template dialog window is closed.
- Click on OK. The dialog window for the templates is also closed.

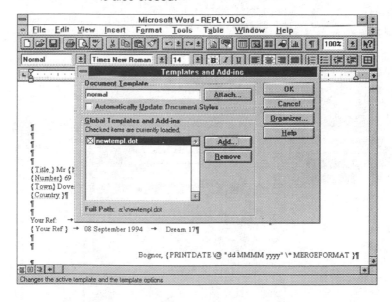

You can now adopt fragments of text from this template by opening the *Edit* menu and selecting *AutoText*.

12.6   Editing text fragments

We shall illustrate how to edit text fragments by altering the Hawkins text fragment. Proceed as follows to include the well-known political philosopher Screaming Jay in the text fragment instead of cousin Coleman:

Example
We shall open a new document based on the New-templ template. The required alterations are made as follows:

- Type 'Hawkins'.
- Press F3 or click on the Insert text fragment button.
- Change 'Mr C. Hawkins' to 'Mr S.J Hawkins'.
- Select the entire text of the altered text fragment.
- Open the *Edit* menu.
- Select the *AutoText* option.
- Select Hawkins from the list.
- Click on the Add button.
- Affirm the safeguard question.

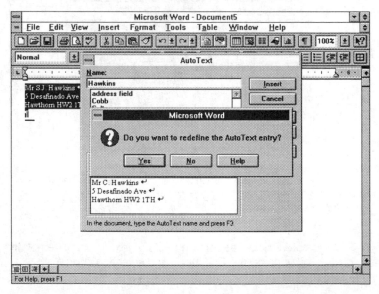

Keep in mind that the alteration has as yet only been made in working memory. Therefore you should confirm that you wish to save the alterations to the template when you close down Word.

12.7 Deleting text fragments

Just for practice, we shall delete the Hawkins text fragment. This is done as follows:

- Open the *Edit* menu.
- Select the *AutoText* option.
- Select Hawkins from the options list.
- Click on the Delete button. Hawkins is removed from the list. Additional fragments can be deleted if required.
- Click on the Close button to close the dialog window.

You cannot delete all text fragments in one go.
Deletion only becomes permanent when you confirm the safeguard question when closing down Word.

12.8 Printing text fragments

If you have a large number of text fragments, it can be convenient to print these for documentation. To do this, the relevant template must be available. In the Print What drop-down list in the Print (*File* menu, *Print*) dialog window, the Document option is the default setting. If you wish to print the text fragments, select AutoText Entries from this list. Subsequently, click on OK to start the printing process. The text fragments are printed in alphabetical order of sequence.

Exercise 12

1   The following text fragment is to be included in the
    NEWTEMPL.DOT template under the name 'Getz'.

    Jot down the commands which are necessary to
    produce this.

    Type the address data.

    _____
    _____
    _____
    _____
    _____
    _____

2   Mr. Gordon has moved house. Change the text
    fragment with his address: Gorlington has become
    Gordonstoun. Note the commands required.

    _____
    _____
    _____
    _____
    _____
    _____
    _____
    _____

Answer 12

1   The following text fragment is to be included in the NEWTEMPL.DOT template under the name 'Getz'.

```
Mr. S. Getz
Shrine Gates
Gettysburg
GT1 2AL Pennsylvania
USA
```

Jot down the commands which are necessary.

Type the address data (use Shift-Enter).
Select the entire text.
Open the Edit menu and select the AutoText option.
Type 'Getz'.
In the Make AutoText Entry Available To section, specify Newtempl.dot.
Click on the Add button.
When the NEWTEMPL.DOT file is closed, confirm the changes.

2   Mr. Gordon has moved house. Change the text fragment with his address: Gorlington has become Gordonstoun. Note the commands required.

Type 'Gordon' and press F3.
Alter the address data.
Select the entire text.
Open the Edit menu and select the AutoText option.
Select the name 'Gordon'.
Select the Add button.
Affirm the safeguard question.

13 Form letters: sending one letter to various addresses

Form letters are letters whose contents are alike for all the recipients. Only the details such as the address and the introduction are different. Word provides a facility for making these quickly and easily. We shall extend our APPOINT document, based on the Newtempl template, to create a form letter which can be sent to all business connections.

Two files are needed to create a form letter. The first file, the *main document*, contains the letter itself along with a number of fields which will be filled with information from the second file, the *data file*, which contains the various personal data.

13.1 The main document

We shall develop the main document from the AP-POINT1.DOC document (created in section 12.5) which made use of the NEWTEMPL template. The text shown below is to be adopted as the contents of the letter in our example.

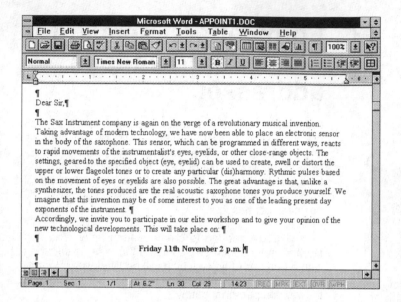

Example

You can use this text but of course you can type your own text for your own form letter. Because you can enter merge fields wherever you wish in your document, it is not necessary to specify any fields. It is however, very convenient if you place an address field on line 8 to fit the window envelope.

■ Move to line 8 and press Ctrl-F9.
■ Type 'address' between the braces.
■ Select the text by pressing F8.
■ Hide it by pressing Ctrl-Shift-H.

We shall enter the place and date registration:

■ Move to line 10 and type the place.
■ Open the *Insert* menu and select *Field*.
■ Select Date and Time in the Categories section.
■ Select PrintDate in the Field Names section.
■ Click on OK.

Type the actual letter text if you have not already done so. Save the document under the name INVIT.DOC.

The personal data will be placed in the address field. In the same way, a field could be created for the letter introduction. If you write letters to friends, ensure that you create a suitable intro instead of the more formal 'Dear Sir/Madam'.

We shall place a field here after the introductory 'Dear' to contain the last name of the recipient:

- Type a space behind 'Dear' and press Ctrl-F9.
- Type the name of the field here, 'LastName'.
- Hide the text by selecting it and pressing Ctrl-Shift-H.

Any fields containing commentary text should be removed because these must not remain in a main document when the actual merging takes place.

13.2 The data file

In order to actually make the form letter, the main document, the letter text has to be linked to a data file. To do this, proceed as follows:

- Open the *Tools* menu.
- Select the *Mail Merge* option. The Mail Merge Helper appears.

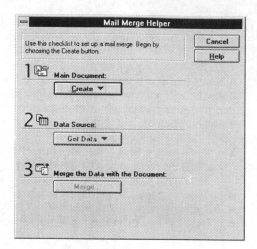

- Click on the first option, Create Main Document. Although the main document already exists, it is only formally recognised when this button has been activated.
- Select the Form Letters option from the options list.

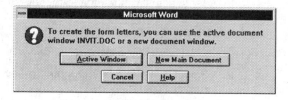

- Click on the Active Window button. The INVIT text is now adopted as the basis for the form letter.
- At 2, click on the Get Data button. You can select an option from the options list to link an existing data file or to create a new one.
- Select the Create Data Source option.

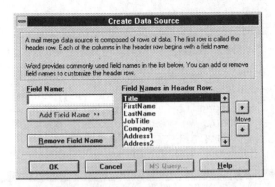

- Select the FirstName option from the Field Names in Header Row list. This list contains many frequently-used field names. Names of fields which you do not use have to be removed. New field names can be added.
- Click on the Remove Field Name button. Remove all the field names except Address1 and LastName (and a Title if you wish to enter more personal details).
- Select the Address1 option from the Field Names in Header Row list. This field name has to be placed in front of the LastName field.
- Click on the button with the arrow pointing upwards in the Move section at the right. The Field names exchange positions.
- Click on OK. The Save Data Source dialog window appears. Specify the name of the data file here.
- Type the name INVIDATA for the data file.
- Click on OK.

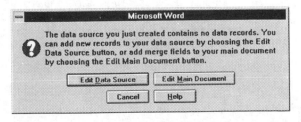

■ Click on the Edit Data Source button.

Now you have linked the INVIDATA data file containing the Intro and Address fields to the main INVIT document. The Data Form dialog window is then opened automatically, so that you can type the data in the corresponding fields. Because we wish to use text fragments we created previously, open the window containing the data file INVIDATA by clicking on the View Source button.

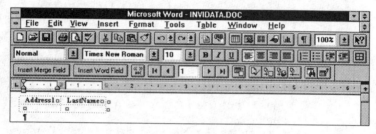

In the table in this window, you can insert the text passages which are to be automatically placed in the Address1 and LastName fields when the form letter is printed. The data which belong to a certain letter are called *records*. In our example, Address1 and LastName form one record; only the data for the LastName have to be typed since the address data are already available as text fragments. Pay attention to the font which has been used to define the text fragments. In order to be able to use the text fragments, link the Newtempl template to the INVIDATA data file. To do this, open the *File* menu, select *Templates*. A dialog window appears. Type the required filename in the Template text box (*A:\newtempl*) and click on OK. You can then enter the text fragments in the Address field.

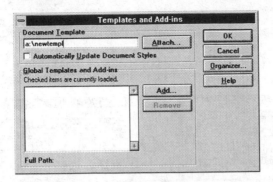

Example

The whole process is as follows. Activate the Print Merge function. Define the INVIT letter as the main document and create the INVIDATA data file. Link the Newtempl template to this document. Increase the width of the columns in the table to accommodate the addresses and the LastNames. Define the contents of the data fields for the merge function according to the steps described below. Specify the data using the same font and font size as the main document.

You can increase the column width directly using the mouse. Drag the right column boundary to the required position. Or open the Cell Height and Width dialog window (*Table* menu) and specify the width using the options in the Column tab sheet.

Proceed as follows to create the table with the data required to make the example form letters.

- Type the name of the text fragment ('Cobb' etc.) and press F3 to insert it, or,
- Open the *Edit* menu, select *AutoText* and select the required name (Cobb etc.). Click on Insert.
- Press Tab to switch to the Intro field.
- Type 'Mr. Cobb' as a personal intro.
- Press Tab to move to a new line for the next record.

- Type 'Coltrane' and press F3 or select the fragment from *AutoText* and click on Insert.
- Press Tab and type 'Mr. Coltrane'.
- Press Tab to begin a new record.
- Enter the other addresses and intros in this way.

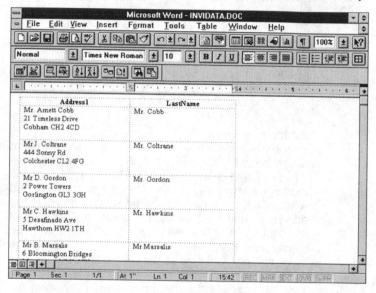

We have now adopted the text fragments and the corresponding intros into the data file, as described above. Save the data file under the name INVIDATA.DOC, just for safety.

In the INVIDATA document window, there is a special toolbar for managing the records.

The buttons have the following significance, from left to right:

Data Form   Switches to the data form.

Manage Fields   Adds, removes or renames fields.

Add New Record Adds a new record.

Delete Record   Deletes an existing record.

Sort Ascending   Sorts records in ascending order.

Sort Descending Sorts records in descending order.

Insert Database   Enables insertion of data from a database, e.g from Access.

Update Fields   Edits data in records.

Find Record   Search for a specific record.

Mail Merge Main Document   Switches to the main document (in our case INVIT.DOC).

Now switch to the main document.

13.3 Inserting data in the main document

A special toolbar (Mail Merge) appears under the Formatting toolbar in the main document. This toolbar has buttons for editing the merge printouts.

These buttons have the following significance, from left to right:

	Insert Merge Field	Inserts a merge field.
	Insert Word Field	Use of a certain data field can be made dependent on a particular condition. Accordingly, you can program the merge, as it were.
	View Merged Data	This displays the main document with the insertions from the data file on the screen.
	**First record, Previous record, Go To record, Next record, Last Record**	Buttons to switch quickly to the relevant record.
	Mail Merge Helper	Switches to the Print Merge dialog window.
	Check for Errors	Checks for any mistakes.
	Merge to New Document	Makes a new document of the merges form letters.
	Merge to Printer	Prints the merges form letters.
	Mail Merge	Make a specific selection of form letters.
	Find Record	Searches for a particular record in the file.
	Edit Data Source	Switches to the data file (Data File dialog window).

The Insert Merge Field button places the various data fields at the relevant position in the main document.

Example
We shall now place the insertion point in front of the paragraph mark on the line where the address is to be placed. Insert the Address1 field here.

- Press Ctrl-Home to move to the beginning of the document.
- Press F11 to move to the first field.
- Press Cursor Right to move to the right of the field.
- Click on the Insert Merge Field button.

When you have clicked on the Merge Field button, an options list appears from which you can select one of the available options. Click on the Address1 option. If the field codes have been activated, {MERGEFIELD Address } will be shown in the document text at the currently active position. If the field codes have not been activated, only { Address } will be shown.

Now enter the LastName field at the position just behind the introduction:

- Press F11 to move to the required field.
- Press Cursor Right to move just outside the field.
- Click on the Insert Merge Field button.
- Select LastName.

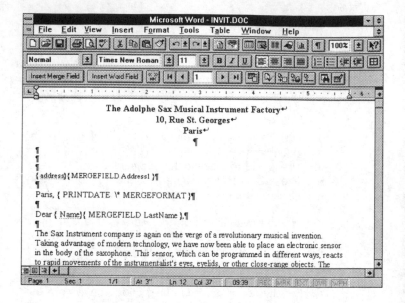

The document should be saved as INVIT2.

13.4 Printing form letters

Checking for and correcting mistakes

The Check for Errors button enables you to check the form letter for any mistakes. In that case, the 'Checking and Reporting Errors' dialog window appears, in which the 'Complete the merge, pausing to report each error as it occurs' option is normally activated. When you have confirmed this by clicking on OK, the main document is linked to the data file and the merged form letters ultimately appear in the Form Letters1 document window. If the inserted data fields do not correspond to those in the data file, the invalid merge fields are displayed. You then have the opportunity to rectify any errors. Errors which are not rectified are indicated at the relevant positions in the form letters. Since the form letters are displayed in a separate window during this check, the 'Merge to New Document' button is scarcely applied. This method provides the same possibilities of correction.

Now check the document for any mistakes and save the automatically created merge document under the name INVIMERG.

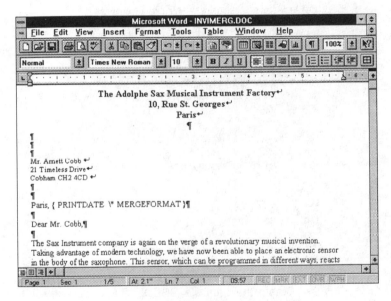

Close the window of the newly created file.

Printing form letters

After all this preparation we can finally print the form letters. To do this, click on the Merge To Printer button (in INVIT.DOC). This opens the familiar Print window. In this dialog window, you can determine whether all the form letters are to be printed or only a selection of these. If the printer is switched on, the letters will be printed, in our case, the five we have created.

Exercise 13

The Adolphe Sax Company regularly checks the payments made by all customers and calculates a credit limit based on these payments. This is the sum for which customers can buy articles without having to pay cash immediately. The payments have to be made within 30 days. Mr Gordon and Mr Hawkins are to receive letters indicating their credit limits.

1   Open a new document to create the following main document with the following text:

Based on the payments throughout the previous years, we have determined that your **credit limit** this year will be $.

We request you, as always, to make payment within 30 days of the invoice date. Payment within 10 days entitles you to a discount of 2% of the sum shown on the invoice.

As a supplement, we enclose our new catalogue and price list.

   Save the text under the name CREDIT.
   Define this text as the main text for the form letter.

2   Create the data file CREDDATA. Include the following fields: Address1, LastName, CreditLimit.

   Mr. Gordon receives a credit limit of $20,000. Mr Hawkins receives a credit limit of $10,000. Save the data file.

3   Insert the Address1, LastName and CreditLimit fields at the appropriate positions in the main document. Save the main document under the name CREDIT2.

4   Check for any errors and create the file for the form letters. Check the letters, Rectify any mis-

takes in either the main document or in the data file. Save the corrected file with the form letters under the name CREDMERG. Print them.

Answer 13

- Open the *File* menu and choose *New*.
- Specify *a:\Newtempl* in the Templates text box.
- Click on OK.
- Open the *Edit* menu and select *AutoText*.
- Insert the heading.
- Move to line 8 and press Ctrl-F9 to create a field. Type 'address' and hide the text by selecting it (F8) and pressing Ctrl-Shift-H.
- Leave a blank line and type the place, Paris.
- Open the *Insert* menu and choose *Field*.
- Select Date and Time and then PrintDate. This ensures that your form letter will always be up-to-date.

You could have imported this line from the APPOINT document. We shall now import a line from the REPLY document to illustrate this.

- Open the REPLY document (*File, Open*).
- Select the line in question:

```
{Title } Mr {Name } G. Clark ¶
{Number} 69 {Street } Charnel Street¶
{Town} Dover {Postal Code} DV3 4HP ¶
{Country }¶
¶
¶
Your Ref    →    Your Letter Dated:    →    Our Ref    →    Our Letter Dated ¶
{Your Ref }  →   08 September 1994    →    Dream 17¶
¶
```

- Select *Edit* and then *Copy*.
- Switch back to your new main document via the *Window* menu.

■ Move the insertion point to the relevant position.
■ Open *Edit* and select *Paste*.

We shall now begin on the letter itself:

■ Type 'Dear' and place a field behind this, { Name }.
■ Type the text of the letter.

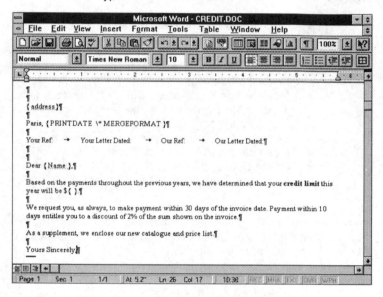

■ Open the *Tools* menu and choose *Mail Merge*.
■ Click on Main Document Create and then on Form Letters.
■ Click on Active Window to specify that the currently active document is to be the main document.
■ Click on Data Source Get Data.
■ Click on Create Data Source.
■ Remove all fields except Address1, LastName.
■ Type CreditLimit in the Field Name box and click on the Add button.
■ Move Address1 to the top of the list using Move.

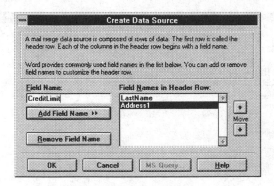

- Click on OK.
- Save the document as CREDDATA.

We shall now continue with the mail merge procedure.

- Click on Edit Data Source to enter the records.
- Click on the View Source button to see the record window.
- Widen the fields by placing the arrow on the dotted line and dragging the frame open.
- Insert the address data using *AutoText* from the *Edit* menu.
- Switch to the other fields by pressing Tab.
- Type the LastName and CreditLimits

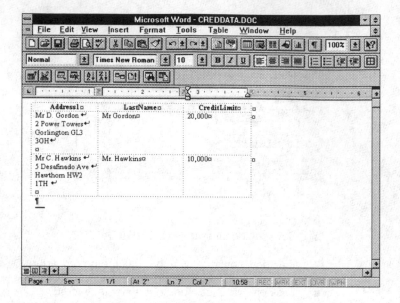

- Save the document.
- Switch to the main document, CREDIT.DOC via the *Window* menu.
- Move the insertion point to the first field, address, by pressing F11.
- Click on the Insert Merge Field button.
- Select Address1.
- Press F11 to move to the Name field.
- Click on the Insert Merge Field button and insert the LastName field.
- Press F11 to move to the dollar sign.
- Click on Insert Merge Field.

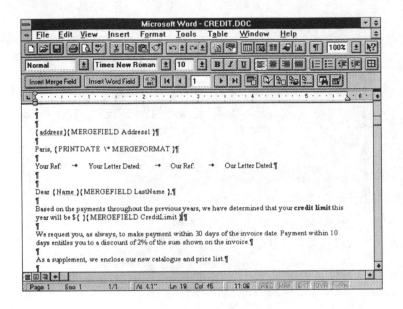

■ Click on the Check for Errors button and then on OK in the subsequent dialog window.

If you have carried out the exercise properly, the result for Mr Gordon should look like this:

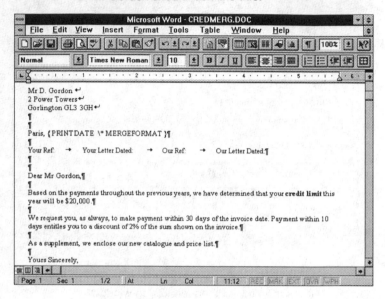

14 Styles

14.1 Changing the Normal style

The Normal style, with which Word opens every new document, uses the Times New Roman, point size 10, as the default font. This is a *proportional font*, which means that the space occupied by the letters differs: an i for instance occupies less space than a w. In addition, the distance between the letters is not fixed; it is adjusted to the space on the line. The point size 10 can only be printed legibly on ink jet or laser printers; for matrix printers, the 12 point size is preferable. Accordingly, the text is also more legible on the screen.

If you have chosen a 12 points font size as the default setting in the Font tab sheet in the Font dialog box (*Format* menu), this will be saved as the default size in the NORMAL.DOT document template. However, alterations to this template should be avoided as much as possible, particularly when several people make use of the same computer. Accordingly, it is better to save any alterations in a separate template, for example in the NEWTEMPL.DOT which we created earlier.

Example
Close any opened document. We shall now open a new document based on the A:NEWTEMPL.DOT template.

- Open the *File* menu.
- Select *New*.
- Specify *a:newtempl* in the Template box.
- Click on OK.

We shall now define the Times New Roman point size 12 as the *default* font for this template. This is done as follows:

- Open the *Format* menu.

- Select the *Font* option.
- Select the Font tab sheet if necessary.
- Select the Times New Roman font.
- Select point Size 12.
- Click on Default. A message box appears.

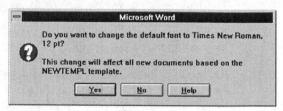

- Reply Yes to the safeguard question.

The alterations to the default font do not come immediately into force; they only apply to any new documents which will be opened, based on this template. Moreover, this alteration has a provisional character. Only when Word is closed down do you get the opportunity to save the alterations in NEWTEMPL.DOT.

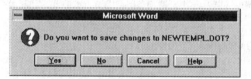

Answer Yes to the subsequent question. The next time you create a document based on NEWTEMPL template, the Times New Roman 12 point font will be the default (Normal) font.

14.2 Applying a style to an existing text

Example

We shall now open the PRINTER text. Because this has been saved with the old Normal document template, this will not appear in the newly defined default font, Times New Roman, 12 points. The alterations to the Newtempl template do not influence this text.

We shall now apply the new template style to this text.

Proceed as follows:

- Open the PRINTER.DOC document.
- Open the *Format* menu.
- Select the *Style Gallery* option.
- Click on the Browse button.
- Type A: in the Template Directory text box or select A from the drives list.
- Click on OK.
- Select Newtempl from the Templates list. The text is displayed the new format in the Preview Of box.
- Click on OK.

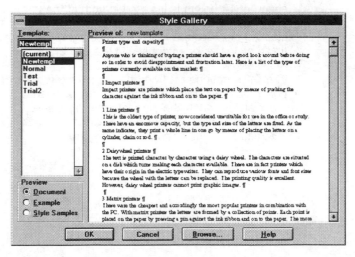

Because the text is automatically formatted using the new Normal default style, the attachment of NEW-TEMPL.DOT has immediate effect on the text. The font size is increased to 12.

14.3   Applying styles to texts

In addition to the Normal style, Word provides a number of other styles which can be used to format text and headings.

Example
We shall apply the 'Heading 3' style to the title of the text.

To do this, open the Style options list at the left of the Formatting toolbar by clicking on the arrow pointing downwards, next to the text box. You can also do this by using the shortcut key combination Ctrl-Shift-S. You can then use the mouse or the cursor keys to select the required style from the list. The Heading 3 style formats the selected text in boldface in the default font. In addition, paragraph formatting also takes place, in which a space of 12 points is inserted in front of the paragraph and a space of 3 points behind the paragraph. A small block is displayed in front of the paragraph to indicate that a style has been applied to this paragraph.

The Style options list from the Formatting toolbar does not contain all the available styles. If you wish to apply other styles, open the *Format* menu and select *Style*. The Style dialog window opens. Click on All Styles in the List box at the bottom of this window.

Example

We shall apply the 'Body Text Indent' style to the paragraphs containing information about the three impact printers and the three non-impact printers.

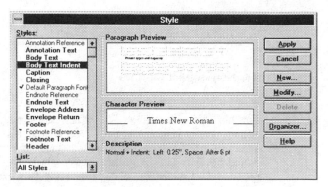

This style is then adopted into the Style list on the Formatting toolbar.

14.4 Creating your own style

By working with the example texts in this book, you have become familiar with formatting characters and paragraphs. You will have realized by now how direct and easy this is. You can make texts quite attractive visually without too much difficulty. The indirect, round-about method of having to open dialog windows via menu options is only necessary to indent paragraphs individually.

Texts often have a left-indentation and a left-aligned first line which often shows a number or summary symbol. You can automatically format these paragraphs using the Bullets and Numbering functions, but these have only limited usage. For instance, you can make a list of points from 1 to 9, but from point 10 onwards, you have to format the paragraphs individually.

For example:

I   Impact printers
Impact printers are printers which ...

   1   Line printers
   This is the oldest type of printer...

   ...
II   Non-impact printers
   ...

For this type of formatting, for which there is no default setting, Word enables you to create your own styles. This makes the formatting of text just as easy as it would be with direct formatting. We shall illustrate the creation and alteration of a style using two examples:

- we shall indent paragraphs by 0.2", excepting the first line
- we shall indent paragraphs with a hanging indentation of 0.5" where, in addition, a left indentation of 0.2" is applied.

We shall use the PRINTER text to illustrate this. First link the heading to the subsequent relevant text by replacing the Hard Return (made by pressing Enter) with a Line Break character (made by pressing Shift-Enter).

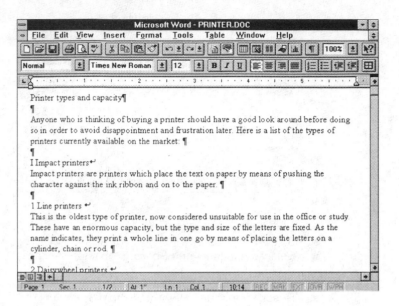

We shall now indent the paragraph which begins with the Roman numeral I. This indentation will be 0.3" but will not apply to the first line which has a hanging indentation. You can compile a formatting profile independently of the text. Because we wish to apply the result to the PRINTER text, this is retained in working memory. Move the insertion point to the paragraph 'I Impact printers'. A hanging indentation is made as follows:

- Open the *Format* menu.
- Select the *Style* option.
- Click on the New Button.
- Enter the name 'Left hanging 3' in the Name text box. The name of the style should indicate the sort of style being applied.
- Select the Paragraph option from the Style Type list.

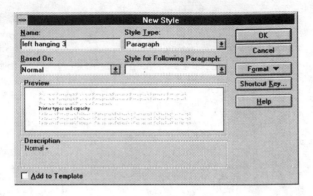

- Click on the Format button.
- Select Paragraph.
- Select the Indents and Spacing tab sheet if necessary.
- Select Hanging from the Special drop-down list.
- Reduce the value in the By box to 0.3".
- Click on OK. The New Style dialog window appears again.
- Click on OK. The Style dialog window appears with the new style activated.
- Click on the Apply button.

Example
We have created the 'Left Hanging 3' style. We shall apply it to the paragraph 'I Impact printers'.

- Select the relevant paragraph.
- Open the Style box on the Formatting toolbar.
- Click on 'left hanging 3'

The paragraph is formatted immediately.

Just for practice, apply the style 'left hanging 7' to the other paragraphs in this document.

Save this under the name PRINSTYL.

The Print Preview of this document will look like this:

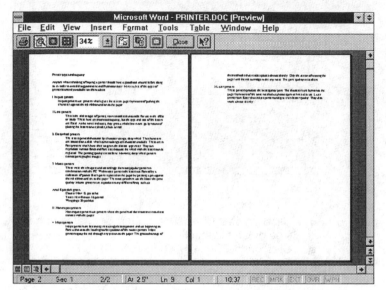

14.5 Including styles in the NEW-TEMPL.DOT template

Styles should be applied to a document template if you want to use this structure frequently. If you quit Word without implementing this application, in the future the style is only available to the document in which you used it.

Example

We shall include the new styles in the Newtempl template. This is done as follows:

- Open the *Format* menu.
- Select the *Style* option.
- Click on the Organizer button.
- Select the Styles tab sheet if necessary.

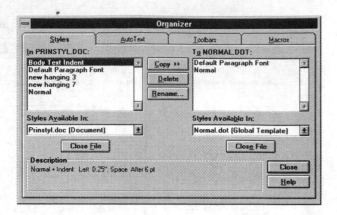

- Click on the Close File button at the right-hand side of the tabsheet.
- Click on the Open File button.
- Type 'a:newtempl.dot' in the File Name text box.
- Click on OK.
- Select the newly-defined styles from the PRIN-STYL.DOC file at the left-hand side of the window.
- Click on the Copy button. The selected formatting templates are then copied to Newtempl.
- Click on the Close button.

Now copy the new style to the Newtempl template and close the document.

- Reply Yes to the question in the subsequent message box.

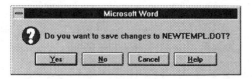

The paragraph styles are available in all
which are created on the Newtempl basis;
in the Style list from the Format toolbar.

14.6 Displaying the style area

Your texts have been subject to a good number of
changes by now. For this reason, it would be convenient to be able to see the formatting details in addition
to your texts. It is possible to display a column in the
left-hand margin showing the details. This is the *Style
Area*. Displaying this is done as follows:

- Open the *Tools* menu.
- Select the *Options* option.
- Select the View tabsheet if necessary.
- Define the width of the formatting column in the
  'Style Area Width' in the Window section. In our
  case, we wish this to be 1".
- Click on OK or press Enter.

Word saves the screen settings and activates them as
soon as you load another document. If you do not want
a formatting area at the left-hand side, specify 0" in the
Style Area width. You can also alter the width of the
formatting area by dragging the dividing line using the
mouse.

14.7 Adopting styles from existing text

In Word it is possible to adopt the character and paragraph formatting features from existing text as a style
and then use it in all situations as required.

Example
In the EMPLOYD2 document, the heading has been
placed in a frame. We shall define this formatting feature in a style called FRAME.

Load the document and place the insertion point at the beginning by pressing Ctrl-Home.

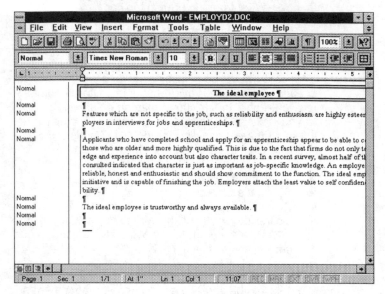

The following commands are necessary to adopt the style from this paragraph:

- Open the *Format* menu.
- Select the *Style* option.
- Click on the New button.
- Type the name FRAME in the text box.
- Click on OK.

Example

We shall now copy the Frame style, which is, up until now, only available in the EMPLOYD2 document, to the Newtempl template. This is done as described in section 14.5. When the EMPLOYD2 document is closed, the Frame style becomes available to all other texts based on the Newtempl template.

Example

We shall open the PRINTER document. Apply the Newtempl document template to this document. Apply the Frame style to any other paragraphs which should be given a frame. Specify a Style Area of 1 inch. Then close the document under the name PRINFRAM.

- Load the PRINTER document.
- Open the *Format* menu.
- Select *Style Gallery*.
- Click on the Browse button.
- Type a: and click on OK to access the Newtempl template on diskette.
- Click on Newtempl and then on OK.
- Click on OK in the Style Gallery window.

The styles in the Newtempl template are now available to the current document.

- Place the insertion point at the required position.
- Click on the Style list on the Formatting toolbar.

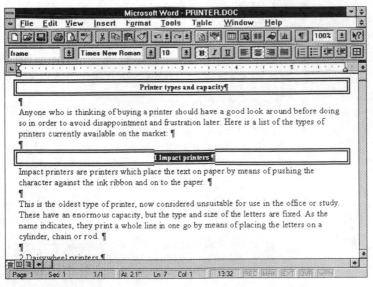

.8   Removing a style

Because styles only become directly available to all texts when you adopt them into the Normal template, this file tends to become larger and larger as time goes on. When you create new texts you are presented with a lengthy list of styles. Accordingly, it is very useful to do a thorough spring cleaning now and again.

Of course, it is advisable not to include certain profiles in the NORMAL.DOT; it is better to store them in a separate .DOT file which is suited to a specific type of text, as we indicated earlier in this section.

Example

Just for practice, we shall remove the 'Left Hanging 7' style from the NEWTEMPL.DOT file. This is done as follows:

- Open the *File* menu and select *Open*.
- Load the NEWTEMPL.DOT file by typing *a:new-templ.dot* in the text box.
- Open the *Format* menu.
- Select the *Style* option.
- Select the 'New Hanging 7' style from the list of styles.
- Click on the Delete button. Reply Yes to the safeguard question which subsequently appears in the message box.
- Click on the Close button.

The style is now removed from working memory. In order to make the deletion definitive, save the NEWTEMPL.DOT file.

Exercise 14

1   Type the text shown below concerning clock speed. Save it under the name CLOCK.

Clock speed

1. A condition of troublefree data processing by the computer is that the components must be geared to one another. This co-ordination is regulated by a crystal in the micro-processor. This crystal ensures a constant clock speed. This clock speed helps determine the system capabilities.

(1) Doubling the clock speed does not automatically lead to a doubling of the capabilities.

(2) When data are read from and written to external storage media, the data are first stored in a buffer in order to adjust the processing speed to the relative tardiness of the heads in the disk drives.

(3) If RAM chips with a low access rate are installed in a computer with a high clock speed, the micro-processor must insert pauses in the processing (wait states).

(4) With computers which can work with several different clock speeds, the highest processing speed is called the turbo mode.

Create styles for the character and paragraph formatting. The formatting profiles are to be stored in the document template CLOCK.DOT. After formatting, the document should look like this:

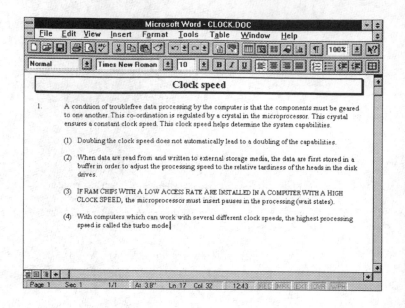

Answer 14

Create a new template, CLOCK.DOT via File, New.

Open a new document using this template.

Type the text without the numbering.

Format the heading via the Bold button, the Center button, 14 pts size.

Draw the box via Format, Borders and Shading. Choose the Shadow box.

Select the first paragraph. Number it via Format, Bullets and Numbering.

Indent it via Format, Paragraph, Hanging indentation.

Select the other paragraphs. Indent them via Format, Paragraph, Left 0.5", Hanging.

Number them via Format, Bullets and Numbering, second box, Modify button, place a bracket in the Text Before button.

> *Define the styles via Format, Style, New, Format,*
> *Paragraph, Apply.*
> *Save and close the document. Save the changes*
> *to CLOCK.DOT.*

If everything has gone smoothly, the result should be identical to that in the figure on the previous page.

Appendix A
Keys to move the insertion point

Key (combination)	Function
Cursor Right	Next character
Cursor Left	Previous character
Cursor Up	Previous line
Cursor Down	Next line
Home	In front of the first character on the line
End	Behind the last character on the line
Ctrl-PgUp	In front of the first character on the first screen page line
Ctrl-PgDn	Behind the last character on the last screen page line
PgUp	One screen page up
PgDn	One screen page down
Ctrl-Cursor Right	In front of the first character of the next word
Ctrl-Cursor Left	In front of the first character of this or the previous word
Ctrl-Cursor Up	In front of the first character of this or the previous paragraph
Ctrl-Cursor Down	In front of the first character of the next paragraph.
Ctrl-Home	To the beginning of the text.
Ctrl-End	To the end of the text.

Appendix B
Selecting passages of text

Key (combination)	Function
F8	Activates the text selection (EXT).
2 x F8	Selects the word in, before or after which the insertion point is located.
3 x F8	Selects the sentence in which the insertion point is located.
4 x F8	Selects the current paragraph.
5 x F8	Selects the entire text.
Shift	Hold down the Shift key and use the cursor keys to select the required passages. Special combinations:
Shift-Ctrl-Cursor Right	Select next word.
Shift-Ctrl-Cursor Left	Select previous word.
Shift-Home	Select text from insertion point to beginning of the line.
Shift-End	Select from the insertion point to the end of the line.
Shift-Ctrl-Cursor Up	From the insertion point one paragraph upwards.
Shift-Ctrl-Cursor Down	From the insertion point one paragraph downwards.
Shift-Ctrl-PgUp	From the insertion point to the first character on the screen.
Shift-Ctrl-PgDn	From the insertion point to the last character on the screen.
Shift-PgUp	From the insertion point back to the previous screen

Shift-PgDn   From the insertion point down
                               to the next screen page.

Shift-Ctrl-Home   From the insertion point to the
                               beginning of the text.

Shift-Ctrl-End   From the insertion point to the
                               end of the text.

Action	Result
Double clicking on a word	Select the word
Clicking in the selection area	Selects the adjacent line
Holding down Ctrl and clicking in a sentence	Selects the sentence
Double clicking in the selection area	Selects the adjacent paragraph
Holding down Ctrl and clicking in the selection area	Selects the entire text

Appendix C
Formatting characters

Key combination	Formatting
Ctrl-Shift-Z	Normal, all character formatting is removed
Ctrl-B	**Bold**
Ctrl-I	*Italics*
Ctrl-Shift-K	SMALL CAPITALS
Ctrl-U	<u>Continuing underlining</u>
Ctrl-Shift-W	<u>Only</u> the <u>words</u> <u>underlined</u>
Ctrl-Shift-D	<u>Double underlining</u>
Ctrl-Shift-Equals sign	Superscript
Ctrl-Equals sign	Subscript
Ctrl-Shift-H	Hidden text
Shift-F3	Display the selection in capitals or small letters, with or without an initial capital; repeat to change back.

Appendix D
Formatting paragraphs

Key combination	Function
Ctrl-J	Justify text
Ctrl-L	Left-align text
Ctrl-R	Right-align text
Ctrl-E	Centre text
Ctrl-1	Single line spacing
Ctrl-2	Double line spacing
Ctrl-5	Line spacing of one and a half
Ctrl-0	Extra line in front of the paragraph
Ctrl-M	Left-indent the paragraph
Ctrl-Shift-M	Right-indent the paragraph
Ctrl-T	Create a hanging indent
Ctrl-Shift-T	Reduce a hanging indent
Ctrl-Q	Remove formatting of the selected paragraph

Appendix E
Other important key combinations

Key (combination)	Function
F1	Help
F3	Insert text fragment
F5	The Go To command from the *Edit* menu
F6	Move the insertion point to the beginning of the next section
F8	Extend the selection
F9	Update field
F11	Move to the next field
Ins	Switch to/from Typeover mode
Del	Delete selected text
Alt-F1	Move to the next field
Alt-Spacebar	Activate the Control menu
Alt-Backspace	Activate Undo from the *Edit* menu
Shift-F1	Activate Help indicator
Shift-F4	Find
Shift-F10	Activate shortcut menu
Shift-Ins	Insert contents of Clipboard
Shift-Del	Copy selection to Clipboard
Shift-Enter	Line break
Ctrl-F9	Insert field
Ctrl-Hyphen	Temporary hyphen
Ctrl-F	Open Find dialog box
Ctrl-Shift-F	Select font
Ctrl-S	Save
Ctrl-Shift-S	Select a style
Ctrl-Shift-P	Select a point size

Ctrl-Ins	Copy selection
Ctrl-V	Insert copied selection
Ctrl-Esc	Activate the Task List
Ctrl-Enter	Specify page break
Ctrl-Backspace	Delete previous word
Ctrl-Shift-Hyphen	Fixed hyphen
Ctrl-Shift-Spacebar	Fixed space

Appendix F
ANSI tabel

Dec	Hex	Char
32	20	(spatie)
33	21	!
34	22	"
35	23	#
36	24	$
37	25	%
38	26	&
39	27	'
40	28	(
41	29	)
42	2A	*
43	2B	+
44	2C	,
45	2D	-
46	2E	.
47	2F	/
48	30	0
49	31	1
50	32	2
51	33	3
52	34	4
53	35	5
54	36	6
55	37	7
56	38	8
57	39	9
58	3A	:
59	3B	;
60	3C	<
61	3D	=
62	3E	>
63	3F	?

Dec	Hex	Char
64	40	@
65	41	A
66	42	B
67	43	C
68	44	D
69	45	E
70	46	F
71	47	G
72	48	H
73	49	I
74	4A	J
75	4B	K
76	4C	L
77	4D	M
78	4E	N
79	4F	O
80	50	P
81	51	Q
82	52	R
83	53	S
84	54	T
85	55	U
86	56	V
87	57	W
88	58	X
89	59	Y
90	5A	Z
91	5B	[
92	5C	\
93	5D	]
94	5E	^
95	5F	_

Dec	Hex	Char
96	60	`
97	61	a
98	62	b
99	63	c
100	64	d
101	65	e
102	66	f
103	67	g
104	68	h
105	69	i
106	6A	j
107	6B	k
108	6C	l
109	6D	m
110	6E	n
111	6F	o
112	70	p
113	71	q
114	72	r
115	73	s
116	74	t
117	75	u
118	76	v
119	77	w
120	78	x
121	79	y
122	7A	z
123	7B	{
124	7C	|
125	7D	}
126	7E	~
127	7F	

Dec	Hex	Char
128	80	
129	81	
130	82	‚
131	83	ƒ
132	84	„
133	85	…
134	86	†
135	87	‡
136	88	ˆ
137	89	‰
138	8A	Š
139	8B	‹
140	8C	Œ
141	8D	
142	8E	
143	8F	
144	90	
145	91	'
146	92	'
147	93	"
148	94	"
149	95	•
150	96	–
151	97	—
152	98	˜
153	99	™
154	9A	š
155	9B	›
156	9C	œ
157	9D	
158	9E	
159	9F	Ÿ

Dec	Hex	Char
160	A0	
161	A1	¡
162	A2	¢
163	A3	£
164	A4	¤
165	A5	¥
166	A6	¦
167	A7	§
168	A8	¨
169	A9	©
170	AA	ª
171	AB	«
172	AC	¬
173	AD	
174	AE	®
175	AF	¯
176	B0	°
177	B1	±
178	B2	²
179	B3	³
180	B4	´
181	B5	µ
182	B6	¶
183	B7	·
184	B8	¸
185	B9	¹
186	BA	º
187	BB	»
188	BC	¼
189	BD	½
190	BE	¾
191	BF	¿

Dec	Hex	Char
192	C0	À
193	C1	Á
194	C2	Â
195	C3	Ã
196	C4	Ä
197	C5	Å
198	C6	Æ
199	C7	Ç
200	C8	È
201	C9	É
202	CA	Ê
203	CB	Ë
204	CC	Ì
205	CD	Í
206	CE	Î
207	CF	Ï
208	D0	Ð
209	D1	Ñ
210	D2	Ò
211	D3	Ó
212	D4	Ô
213	D5	Õ
214	D6	Ö
215	D7	×
216	D8	Ø
217	D9	Ù
218	DA	Ú
219	DB	Û
220	DC	Ü
221	DD	Ý
222	DE	Þ
223	DF	ß

Dec	Hex	Char
224	E0	à
225	E1	á
226	E2	â
227	E3	ã
228	E4	ä
229	E5	å
230	E6	æ
231	E7	ç
232	E8	è
233	E9	é
234	EA	ê
235	EB	ë
236	EC	ì
237	ED	í
238	EE	î
239	EF	ï
240	F0	ð
241	F1	ñ
242	F2	ò
243	F3	ó
244	F4	ô
245	F5	õ
246	F6	ö
247	F7	÷
248	F8	ø
249	F9	ù
250	FA	ú
251	FB	û
252	FC	ü
253	FD	ý
254	FE	þ
255	FF	ÿ

Appendix G
ASCII tabel

Dec	Hex	Chr	Dec	Hex	Chr	Dec	Hex	Chr	Dec	Hex	Chr
0	0		32	20		64	40	@	96	60	`
1	1	☺	33	21	!	65	41	A	97	61	a
2	2	☻	34	22	"	66	42	B	98	62	b
3	3	♥	35	23	#	67	43	C	99	63	c
4	4	♦	36	24	$	68	44	D	100	64	d
5	5	♣	37	25	%	69	45	E	101	65	e
6	6	♠	38	26	&	70	46	F	102	66	f
7	7	•	39	27	'	71	47	G	103	67	g
8	8	◘	40	28	(	72	48	H	104	68	h
9	9	○	41	29	)	73	49	I	105	69	i
10	A	◙	42	2A	*	74	4A	J	106	6A	j
11	B	♂	43	2B	+	75	4B	K	107	6B	k
12	C	♀	44	2C	,	76	4C	L	108	6C	l
13	D	♪	45	2D	-	77	4D	M	109	6D	m
14	E	♫	46	2E	.	78	4E	N	110	6E	n
15	F	☼	47	2F	/	79	4F	O	111	6F	o
16	10	►	48	30	0	80	50	P	112	70	p
17	11	◄	49	31	1	81	51	Q	113	71	q
18	12	↕	50	32	2	82	52	R	114	72	r
19	13	‼	51	33	3	83	53	S	115	73	s
20	14	¶	52	34	4	84	54	T	116	74	t
21	15	§	53	35	5	85	55	U	117	75	u
22	16	▬	54	36	6	86	56	V	118	76	v
23	17	↨	55	37	7	87	57	W	119	77	w
24	18	↑	56	38	8	88	58	X	120	78	x
25	19	↓	57	39	9	89	59	Y	121	79	y
26	1A	→	58	3A	:	90	5A	Z	122	7A	z
27	1B	←	59	3B	;	91	5B	[	123	7B	{
28	1C	∟	60	3C	<	92	5C	\	124	7C	¦
29	1D	↔	61	3D	=	93	5D	]	125	7D	}
30	1E	▲	62	3E	>	94	5E	^	126	7E	~
31	1F	▼	63	3F	?	95	5F	_	127	7F	△

Dec	Hex	Chr	Dec	Hex	Chr	Dec	Hex	Chr	Dec	Hex	Chr
128	80	Ç	160	A0	á	192	C0	└	224	E0	α
129	81	ü	161	A1	í	193	C1	┴	225	E1	β
130	82	é	162	A2	ó	194	C2	┬	226	E2	Γ
131	83	â	163	A3	ú	195	C3	├	227	E3	π
132	84	ä	164	A4	ñ	196	C4	─	228	E4	Σ
133	85	à	165	A5	Ñ	197	C5	┼	229	E5	σ
134	86	å	166	A6	ª	198	C6	╞	230	E6	μ
135	87	ç	167	A7	º	199	C7	╟	231	E7	τ
136	88	ê	168	A8	¿	200	C8	╚	232	E8	Φ
137	89	ë	169	A9	⌐	201	C9	╔	233	E9	Θ
138	8A	è	170	AA	¬	202	CA	╩	234	EA	Ω
139	8B	ï	171	AB	½	203	CB	╦	235	EB	δ
140	8C	î	172	AC	¼	204	CC	╠	236	EC	∞
141	8D	ì	173	AD	¡	205	CD	═	237	ED	ø
142	8E	Ä	174	AF	«	206	CE	╬	238	EE	∈
143	8F	Å	175	B0	»	207	CF	╧	239	FF	∩
144	90	É	176	B1	▓	208	D0	╨	240	F0	≡
145	91	æ	177	B2	▓	209	D1	╤	241	F1	±
146	92	Æ	178	B3	█	210	D2	╥	242	F2	≥
147	93	ô	179	B4	┤	211	D3	╙	243	F3	≤
148	94	ö	180	B5	┤	212	D4	╘	244	F4	⌠
149	95	ò	181	B6	╢	213	D5	╒	245	F5	⌡
150	96	û	182	B7	╖	214	D6	╓	246	F6	÷
151	97	ù	183	B8	╕	215	D7	╫	247	F7	≈
152	98	ÿ	184	B9	╣	216	D8	╪	248	F8	°
153	99	Ö	185	BA	║	217	D9	┘	249	F9	•
154	9A	Ü	186	BB	╗	218	DA	┌	250	FA	·
155	9B	¢	187	BC	╝	219	DB	█	251	FB	√
156	9C	£	188	BD	╜	220	DC	▄	252	FC	ⁿ
157	9D	¥	189	BE	╛	221	DD	▌	253	FD	²
158	9E	₧	190	BF	┐	222	DE	▐	254	FE	■
159	9F	ƒ	191	C0	┐	223	DF	▀	255	FF	

Index

PRISMA **COMPUTER COURSE**

also in this series:

Computer Course
Lotus 1-2-3 for Windows

No other package has attained such world-wide distribution as Lotus 1-2-3. In fact, throughout the world, there are more than twenty million users of this package, which has led to it being regarded as the industrial norm. The many functions available and the ease of operation have resulted in this program being the market leader in almost all sales statistics.

This book deals with the Windows version of this program package. Lotus 1-2-3 for Windows contains all the features of the current DOS version, but also provides the convenience of operation and the display options of the Windows user-interface, along with the special possibilities of exchanging data with other applications running under Windows.

This book presents a structured course in working with Lotus 1-2-3 for Windows. It provides everything required to master the instructions, functions and additional facilities of the package.

ISBN 1 85365 390 X   pages 308

PRISMA COMPUTER COURSE

also in this series:

Computer Course
Windows 3.0 and 3.1

Microsoft's Windows 3.1 is the new standard in graphical user interfaces. The windows environment can be installed on all computers that work with the MS-DOS operating system and are equipped with an Intel 80286 or more powerful processor. Windows adapts automatically to its hardware environment (graphics adaptor, type of processor, amount of memory). Consequently Windows offers the best possible performance on every system.

Windows applications work in a consistent way as far as the user interface is concerned. It is very easy to merge text, numeric data and graphics, as well as exchanging data between the various Windows applications.

This book is a structured, practical course in working with Windows 3.1, Windows applications and the computer. Furthermore, it discusses the improvements of the new Windows version, such as the improved DOS application support, the new TrueType fonts and the OLE technique (Object Linking and Embedding).

ISBN 1-85365-345-4   pages 304

PRISMA COMPUTER COURSE

also in this series:

Computer Course
WordPerfect for Windows

In a relatively short time, WordPerfect has become the most widespread word processing program in the entire world. And since the introduction of Windows 3.1, this graphic user shell has become enormously popular. The advantages are obvious - the user can see the result of each action directly and immediately on the screen.

WordPerfect has now been made even easier - the graphic style aids the selection of options and commands; visual presentation replaces memory work, giving the user a constant picture of all the running processes.

This book provides step-by-step guidance to all aspects of the program, supplementing the information with many examples. Practical and clear exercises are also included so that the user can test his/her progress through each of the learning stages.

ISBN 1 85365 570 5   pages 240